SKOL

It must be the taste.

First published in hardback in Great Britain in 2008 by
Orion Books
an imprint of the Orion Publishing Group Ltd
Orion House, 5 Upper St Martin's Lane,
London WC2H 9EA
An Hachette Livre UK Company

3 5 7 9 10 8 6 4

A CIP catalogue record for this book is available from the British Library.

ISBN: 978 0 7528 9887 2

Printed in Spain by Cayfosa

The Orion Publishing Group's policy is to use papers that are natural, renewable and recyclable and
made from wood grown in sustainable forests. The logging and manufacturing processes are expected
to conform to the environmental regulations of the country of origin.

Every effort has been made to fulfil requirements with regard to reproducing copyright material.
The author and publisher will be glad to rectify any omissions at the earliest opportunity.

www.orionbooks.co.uk

WARNING!

The Rough Pub Guide is a celebration of the great British boozer.
As will be obvious from the text it is a humorous look at the pubs we
love, and inclusion within *The Rough Pub Guide* is not a criticism of the
premises featured. On the contrary, we think they're all great. As will also
be obvious, *The Rough Pub Guide* has no connection whatsoever with
either the Rough Guides, the *Good Beer Guide* or any other publication.

'YOU MEET A BETTER CLASS OF PEOPLE IN PUBS'
– OLIVER REED –

FANCY

Us too. The trouble is, finding a decent pub these days isn't easy. Just look around you. On every high street, enormo-dome theme pubs cater for Binge Britain's endless Happy Hour, where the music's too loud and the taxi home comes courtesy of St John's Ambulance or the local constabulary.

Out in the country and in cities which survived the Blitz, ancient locals are closing down faster than you can ring 'Last Orders'. In their place bars selling guinea fowl sausages for fifteen quid because the ludicrous bloke in the kitchen thinks he's Gordon Ramsay.

In short, the Great British boozer is an endangered species, dismissed as an irrelevance by the same people who told us the Sinclair C5 was the future of car travel.

Welcome then, to *The Rough Pub Guide*, a celebration of the fifty most extraordinary drinking experiences in the UK. In these pages

A PINT?

You'll find psychotic inner city pit-stops, the psychedelic cider still favoured by Joe Strummer (R.I.P.), pubs stuck on craggy islands and even a bar in a converted public toilet.

To qualify, these premises had to satisfy some tough criteria. Firstly, they had to have been open at least ten years. Wherever possible, they had to have fixtures and fittings which hadn't seen a lick of paint since the war (the Crimean War, that is). Finally, they needed to boast a maverick energy or independent spirit sadly lacking in these days of homogenised chain pubs and gastromakeovers. The results, in best pub quiz tradition, appear here in reverse order.

Both a countdown to pub nirvana and a celebration of what makes these islands great. *The Rough Pub Guide* is a woozy outing round the British Isles as seen through a froth-stained pint glass.

Time, gentlemen please, to meet the landlords that time forgot...

FOREWORD

Outside, a lurid yellow poster reads: 'Police Incident: Serious Assault took place here. Did You See Anything?' By the door a Golf GTI lurches forward, convulsing to the hip-hop belching from its speakers.

Other than for a smattering of pensioners nursing pints, the pub is empty. The atmosphere is so dead Burke & Hare would get a hard-on.

On the dance-floor a teenage barmaid giggles to herself as she jack-knifes a punter's motorised wheelchair against the 'Who Wants To Be A Millionaire?' quiz machine.

'You daft bint,' barks its owner mirthlessly. 'You've pranged the Roller.'

At the bar two blokes discuss their investment portfolios.

'I'm totally broke, bruv,' says one.

'Fucking Murray Mint mate,' says the other. He raises his pint in a mock toast. 'Happy days.'

A man appears to my left. 'So what do *you* want from life?' he says.

As the question hangs in the air, I make a quick appraisal of my interrogator. A pub veteran, he wears his double chins as medals, his glazed expression like a battle-weary officer who never quite left the trenches. Should I tell him that we're travelling the country on a mission to uncover the rough diamonds of the pub world? That, unless something is done, pubs like this will become the modern-day equivalent of churches – abandoned temples hopelessly out of synch with the times?

'A pint of Fosters,' I say.

It's the right answer.

He nods agreement and gestures to the barmaid.

HAPPY
HOUR
MON - FRI
11AM -
5PM

50 THE JAGGY THISTLE
49 THE ROYAL STANDARD
48 THE PRINCE OF WALES
47 THE FOX & HOUNDS
46 TAFARN SINC
45 THE VICTORIA
44 NELLIE'S
43 THE BOOT
42 THE CROOKED HOUSE
41 FAGANS

THE JAGGY THISTLE

10–12 YORK STREET, BLACKPOOL, FY1 5AQ

THE MOST SCOTTISH PUB IN BRITAIN. IT JUST HAPPENS TO BE IN ENGLAND.

The Jaggy Thistle: never has a pub been better named. The alcoholic equivalent of a hard-wire brush up the backside, The Jaggy is a redbrick bunker designed for full-tilt boozing where, if you're lucky, you'll only leave with a skin rash.

Ask for a mineral water and you'll have your sexuality questioned. Enquire if butternut squash risotto is on the menu and you could be dining at Blackpool Infirmary. But at The Jaggy, they're only doing what it says on the tin. A notice

on the door reads: 'Not For The Faint-Hearted', and anyone advertising the fact they couldn't tell Kenny Dalglish from Jimmy Krankie is, frankly, asking to leave via the (tartan) windows.

'You won't get any bother here unless you go looking for it,' says long-term regular Ian Macleod. 'I've been to Tartan Army events all over the world, and this is the most patriotic Scottish pub you'll ever find.'

Sadly, The Jaggy no longer hosts the female mud-wrestling nights captured for posterity on 'Mucky Mud Maidens', but the place retains a firecracker energy. At weekends punters regularly indulge in seventeen-hour drinking sessions with one eye permanently on the karaoke corner.

Fancy a quick rendition of 'Swing Low, Sweet Chariot'? Now that really would take a braveheart. ☩

THE ROYAL STANDARD

EAST BEACH STREET, HASTINGS,
EAST SUSSEX, TN34 3AP

LET'S DO THE TIMEWARP AGAIN.

Hastings. The last resting place of Aleister Crowley, 'the wickedest man in the world'. The town that cruelly robbed us of Rod Hull – and, with him, Emu – when he fell from his roof trying to fix a dodgy TV aerial; the place where the life of tragic rock mum Paula Yates began. Not exactly the Magic Kingdom.

The low rumble of 'Tusk' by Fleetwood Mac greets me as I enter The Royal Standard. The signs are all there: 'Shirts Must Be Worn At All Times'; 'Meat Raffle on Monday – £1'. A fly-poster announces the live return of Shaun Williamson, a.k.a. Barry from Eastenders. By the bar, a giant dog strains at the leash, its tattooed owner struggling to control it. Like a crisp-crazed Hound of the Baskervilles, the half-masticated remainders of a bag of Walkers salt &vinegar fall from its slathering jaws. I watch as a sixty-year-old woman in white Sta-Prest trousers bends down to pet the beast. You can clearly make out that she is wearing an orange thong. A ten-year-old pot man, face as world weary as a pensioner, drifts by.

Through the window, I can see a queue snaking outside the tattoo parlour next door. Plucking up courage, I ask a local what passes for entertainment round here. Didn't I know? Chicory Tip are playing live in five minutes.

They of course, turn out to be great.

Close your eyes, and in The Royal Standard, it really is 1972. ☦

THE PRINCE OF WALES

23 BRIDGE ROAD, EAST MOLESEY, SURREY, KT8 9EU

HOME OF THE CAMPAIGN FOR SURREAL ALE.

Some pubs have a reputation for being mad. From Penzance to Pittordrie, the mere mention of certain boozers will have the locals shaking their heads and muttering into their John Smith's about the lunatic fringe who congregate there.

Others, however, have madness thrust upon them. Such is the case with The Prince of Wales. Like a boozy David Banner, most of the time the POW is an unassuming local tucked away in the Surrey commuter belt. It's only when it's called into use as borough HQ for the Monster Raving Loony Party that it explodes into an Incredible Hulk of pub weirdness.

If you roll up during their annual Mad Hatters' Tea Party, you'll find youself sharing bar space with Professor Retard, Banana Man and Mad Cow-Girl. Cast an eye over the minutes, and you might get a scoop on initiatives ranging from the banning of coat hangers to the repatriation of all traffic wardens to Iraq.

'Every five years 650 of the most uptight people in the country win heats in local competitions and then have a big shout-off in some large building by the Thames,' explains Jason 'Chinners' Chinnery (Shadow Minister of Fortean Spinning & Bouncing). 'We counteract that by having our victory party the night before the election.'

Anyone doubting the MRLP's suitability for government should note the party's radical plans to tackle binge drinking.

'The current licensing laws are causing problems,' says Chinners. 'Because of this, we plan to extend opening hours to thirty-two hours a day.' ✠

THE FOX & HOUNDS

216 NEW ROAD, CROXLEY GREEN, HERTFORDSHIRE, WD3 3HH

LAGER THAN LIFE: FOOTBALL FANTASY PUB.

In the opening lines of *The Hitchhiker's Guide to the Galaxy*, a girl in Rickmansworth experiences a blinding moment of euphoria. Before she has a chance to act upon it, a terrible catastrophe occurs. For England fans at the nearby Fox & Hounds, it's a feeling they know all too well.

Drinking is made simple here. At the bar, Carling, Fosters and Stella are automatic selections, while multiple screens ensure that even Zaphod Beebelbrox could get a good view.

During major tournaments, terracing is even installed in the balcony bar to provide that 'I was there' frisson as the final England penalty is blazed wide.

Sport-hating beer bores should probably drink elsewhere, especially on St George's Day, when the pub's homemade flag (see right) gets an airing. But the F&H isn't only for myopic England fans.

'We once had a customer called Dennis who used to come in with a parrot on his shoulder,' says manager Kate O'Neill. 'And one day someone came in and started disembowelling fish on the counter, much to our horror.'

The Fox & Hounds: England fans might get upset, but the fish are gutted. ✠

TAFARN SINC

PRESILI, ROSEBUSH,
WALES, SA66 7QU

A GREAT PLACE TO GET OUT OF YOUR (SIGNAL) BOX …

When Russell T. Davies decided to reboot the Dr Who franchise in his native Wales, little did he realise that there were already families of Autons lurking down in the farthest corners of the Principality. Built back in 1876, Tafarn Sinc (Zinc Pub in translation) is a corrugated iron shed painted a ferrous red. It was originally a hotel at the end of a long-gone train line built quickly by the Victorians in the hope that the area might catch on as a tourist destination. Now, in a fantastically eccentric tribute to the long-gone railway, a replica platform has been created outside the pub. On it, a gathering of sinister mannequins waits come rain or shine, for a train that will never arrive. The occasional steam-age whistle you hear is played through a replica signal box,

adding another layer to the eerie Whovian atmosphere of the place.

Thankfully, our inanimate friends are absent from the inside of the Tafarn, meaning that you can enjoy an un-menaced pint in the warmth of the bar with friendly Welsh-speaking locals. A wood-burning stove takes pride of place, while local memorabilia covers the walls and ceilings. On the bar, Cwrw Tafarn Sinc, a beer brewed specially for the pub, sits alongside other fine beers from Cardiff's Brains brewery. It's only when you've had a few and get up to leave that you're reminded of the weirdness outside. On leaving and heading back towards relative sanity, you half expect to see a wild-eyed David Tennant emerging from a blue police box gesticulating wildly at the bar staff with his sonic screwdriver. C'mon there, you might be a Time Lord, but you pay cash for your bloody beer round here mun… ✠

Wetherspoon's pubs certainly have their critics but, really, they are an essential part of Rough Pub Britain – vast alco-pit stops out there, waiting for your custom, on every British high street (the chain numbers 696 pubs at the time of writing). These temples to the common man offer cheap, well-kept booze from morning 'til night – in fact, on a recent visit to the Newcastle-under-Lyme branch, groups of men sat imbibing pints of lager at 9.45 on a Thursday morning. These men are the true denizens of Rough Pub country, they are its labour force, out there working the coalface and putting in the hours while you and I are bleary eyed, hammering down over-priced coffees, trying to make sense of the day that lies ahead of us…

I digress. The Wetherspoon pub chain is clearly run by someone who loves beer in all its forms. The J.D. Wetherspoon chain was the brainchild of Tim Martin, a 6ft 6in mulleted Euro-sceptic who named his company after an old schoolmaster who once told him he 'would not amount to anything'. The J.D. part, fantastically, comes from his favourite character from The Dukes of Hazzard. The pubs are often polish-ups of listed interiors – in the case of the Holloway Road branch in North London, the Savoy Cinema was saved from demolition and resurrected as a booze palace. This environment is conducive to drinking and little else – there is no music other than the occasional chirrup of a mobile phone or the payout of a jackpot machine (the Wetherspoon's exception to this rule is the younger, glitzier Lloyds No.1 sub-chain where music is played – loud). Drink is the respectable side of cheap – sheer volumes shifted over the chain mean that bulk buying brings with it quality grog at cheaper prices (same as the Sam Smith's chain of boozers, where you can still find a pint for under two quid in the West End if you know where to look). Food plays a minor role, with two-for-one meal deals – burger, chips and a pint – for under a fiver, themed nights (e.g. Tuesday curry club) and the occasional regional twists, all there with the express purpose of keeping you fed to keep you drinking. The perfect scenario really.

At the end of the day, the thing that really works about a J.D. Wetherspoon pub, the thing we love, is the brilliant consistency – the beer is good and it's cheap; it's open a few more hours than you could ever need; the food is decent, plentiful and also cheap; it's not full of wankers – that much is the same wherever you go. Before writing this book, we didn't really have a route map of the great pubs of the United Kingdom that told us where was good and where was, frankly, terrifying. Even clutching CAMRA guides, you run the risk of walking into places that resemble the bar out of the first *Star Wars* film on scrumpy delivery day. In times when you're faced with the Pints That Time Forgot, fearful for your life, your sanity or your bowels (that'll be the scrumpy then), you can pretty much guarantee that the nearest Wetherspoon's will more or less be the same as the one local to your own, probably down to the same identikit old blokes propping up the bar with half a pint of mild in hand. For all those reasons, we love a Wetherspoon's – from Land's End to John O'Groats. See you there for curry club! ⊹

THE VICTORIA

WHITWICK ROAD, COALVILLE, LEICS, LE67 3FA

IF YOU LOVE THE SOUND OF NAPALM DEATH IN THE MORNING.

If the Midlands can be described as the home of heavy metal, then The Victoria – a.k.a. Vic's Biker Pub – must surely be its slightly scuzzy front room.

In the back bar, faded gig posters tell of boozy bacchanals starring tribute bands ranging from Ozzmosis and ZZ Stop to, erm, Isaac Hunt. On the pub's website, images of gleaming Kawasakis jostle with smoking bum-cracks and American Hot-Rods where the attention is naturally drawn to 'Cleavage Corner'.

'It's a bikers pub, but we get plenty of truckers, too,' says genial landlord John Commons. 'When it gets really busy, I let people camp in the back garden.'

If the thought of waking up next to a hungover Vulcan Rider doesn't appeal,

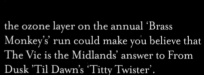

the ozone layer on the annual 'Brass Monkey's' run could make you believe that The Vic is the Midlands' answer to From Dusk 'Til Dawn's 'Titty Twister'.

But the run is for charity and trouble here is unheard of. On New Year's Eve, revellers looking to end the night with a bang can even try on 'The Helmet Of Doom': a crash helmet converted into an

THE VICTORIA BIKERS PUB

COALVILLE . LEICESTERSHIRE . ENGLAND

NELLIE'S
(A.K.A. THE WHITE HORSE)

22 HENGATE, BEVERLEY, EAST YORKSHIRE, HU17 8BL

WORTH A TRIP TO HULL AND BACK.

All pubs are refuges. They are front rooms that you will never be able to find in a normal house. They occupy that magical place between office and home, between the day and the evening, between mates and the wife. This is not a new behavioural pattern. Our ancestors also knew a thing or two about this precious and important half-time, this time for liquid reflection.

The White Horse in Beverley (which is only ever referred to as Nellie's in honour of the landlady of fifty years) has been providing this sanity-saving service for hundreds of years. No records exist, but if you have the pleasure of sinking a few in Nellie's you might well be joined by the ghosts of Vikings who raped and pillaged their way across this part of the world in the ninth century.

Lots of pubs aspire to the Victorian ideal of gaslight and mahogany, but Nellie's is the genuine article. It is still lit by gaslight: the perfect venue for Sherlock Holmes to present to Dr Watson a cocaine-amplified thesis concerning a grisly local murder.

It's important to bear in mind that Nellie's is no theme park, however. As a sixth former obsessed with Fugazi and punk rock, Beverley could be a dangerous place. Nellie's always offered sanctuary from the harsh and often-violent rural northern Friday night populated by the Rottweiler-faced young farmers who lived locally. On school days, we would even go there to watch Neighbours at lunchtime in the pool room after double history. ✚

THE BOOT

116 CROMER STREET,
LONDON, WC1H 8BS

'CARRY ON' STAR KENNETH WILLIAMS' LOCAL.

The Boot has long been a stopping-off point for travellers alighting from King's Cross station – a sickly red and yellow beacon for those needing to steady the nerves following a close encounter with British Rail.

On entering, a man looks up, and, staring me in the eye, burps loudly. Is it a greeting or a warning? It's hard to say, but I nod anyway. Seconds later his mobile rings – playing the Rocky theme – and he's off into the doorway for a heated discussion.

'It's all down to that c**t from Dagenham!' he fumes, before the door slams shut, leaving me in the warm fug of the interior.

On the TV, 'Mysterious Girl' by Peter Andre plays on what seems to be a continuous loop. On the walls, framed photographs tell of The Boot's more illustrious past. A tavern since 1630, it was a regular boozing destination for Charles Dickens, who mentioned it in Barnaby Rudge. More recently, Kenneth Williams – who grew up nearby on Marchmont Street – often propped up the bar with a gin and tonic. Why there's a picture of Lee 'Six Million Dollar Man' Majors on the wall, a stuffed kangaroo by the bar or an exercise bike in the ladies is less obvious.

But then, at The Boot, no one asks any questions. This is the anti-Cheers, a place to wallow in the fact that no one knows your name. Hours pass. 'Mysterious Girl' keeps playing. Occasionally lost tourists enter and, gauging the mood, swiftly abandon plans to gawp at a statue in St Pancras.

I silently raise a toast to the spiritual home of Carry On Drinking. ⚓

THE CROOKED HOUSE

CROOKED HOUSE LANE, HIMLEY, NR DUDLEY, WEST MIDLANDS, DY3 4DA

WONKY CHÂTEAUX: EXPECT HIGH SPIRIT LEVELS...

Most seasoned drinkers will be used to finding themselves staggering through public houses, banging into walls they are sure weren't there five minutes before. This is usually followed by a few terse words from the landlord and an early bus ride home. Thankfully, this is (most often) not the case with The Crooked House.

Originally known in the nineteenth century as The Glynne Arms, the building suffered so badly from local coal-mining subsidence that it began to fall into a hole. Now, one side of the pub lies four feet lower than the other, giving it a boozy Lewis Carroll-esque effect, less 'Through The Looking Glass' and more 'Through The Pint Pot'. Walls stand at 45-degree angles and corridors rise when they should fall. Place your glass on certain tables in the pub and it will appear to slide uphill. Place a pork scratching on the floor and watch it crawl away backwards (possibly). How the resident ghost – Polly the serving maid – copes, we'll never know. Basically, here you'll experience those kicking-out-time hallucinations without touching a drop. The Crooked House – because, sometimes, you need to know that it's not just you... ✠

FAGANS

69 BROAD LANE, SHEFFIELD, S1 4BS

THEY NEVER PROMISED YOU A BEER GARDEN.

'This is the best pub in Sheffield,' says the minicab driver as we pull up next to an asphalt-coloured bunker next to a building site. 'Not that you'd know it to look at it.'

If any pub reflects the spirit of a city, it's Fagans. A local fixture since the late nineteenth century, it's provided more community service than Naomi Campbell. Originally called The Barrel it was rechristened in 1985 in honour of former licensee Joe Fagan – who manned the pumps for a full thirty-seven years. The pub is now the habitat of current landlord Tom Boulding, who has been here ever since.

Dimly-lit in mid-afternoon Fagans possesses a Marie Celeste-like stillness. A photo of Henry Hall – aka 'The Fighting Milkman Of Sky Edge' – is a reminder of how boxing heroes conducted themselves before Prince Naseem, while oil paintings of RAF bombers remind patrons they could be drinking from Steins in another life.

The back room plays host to a legendary jam session that has attracted everyone from Jools Holland to Richard Hawley, but at Fagans they don't go on about it.

Even the smoking ban doesn't seem to bother landlord Tom.

'Nothing's changed,' he shrugs. 'In fact, people prefer to drink here without a nicotine marinade.'

The one concession to exoticism is a sign above the door in Japanese that reads: 'We install and service hangovers'. ✝

ARE YOU BEING SERVED?

A ROUND-UP OF THE BEST PUBS ON TELEVISION.

If only pubs in the real world were as immune to change as the Queen Vic or the Rovers (Bette Lynch, right). Most pubs on TV, however, are about as much fun as sharing a half of mild with Shadrach Dingle or ploughing your way through a plate of Betty's Hotpot. Thankfully, there have been several exceptions over the years, those imaginary beerodromes written with enough warmth and respect as to make Logie Baird proud. Here we present the five pubs on the box that truly justify the licence fee.

5. THE KEBAB & CALCULATOR
(THE YOUNG ONES)

Introduced by Mike in the episode 'Boring' with the words: 'We're bored stupid and we've got nothing to eat, I think the time has come for us to go to the pub,' the K&C (filmed at The Cock O' The North in Bristol – one of only two circular pubs in Britain) brilliantly reflects an early '80's climate where young drinkers were tolerated rather than tempted. Service comes with a scowl, a round (a glass of water, a Baby Cham for Vyv) costs £25, and the carpets are as threadbare as a student fridge at Christmas.

It's a snapshot of a distant age, before alcopops and wheat beers, where an option of Smoky Bacon crisps seemed decadent. To ram the point home, Madness perform to an audience apparently superglued to their chairs.

Welcome to the 'House of Fun'.

4. THE WINCHESTER CLUB
(MINDER)

A magnet for 'every low-life villain on the manor' according to Inspector Chisholm (the superb Patrick Malahide), The Winchester Club exists as its own nation state – a subterranean principality designed for shady deals where honour among thieves vanishes the second your collar's felt.

'My Gawd, they've nicked Pongo. I only hope it's something very serious and nothing to do with me,' says a perturbed Arthur after hearing the latest on the bar-top dog and bone. In long-suffering landlord Dave, this smoky safehouse has a licensee to warm the heart of Al Murray. Reluctant to leave his post behind the bar, a trip upstairs is unwelcome. Visiting France, unpalatable. 'Dodgy water, sawn-off toilets and Plod with guns,' he grumbles at the thought. Pugnacious, loyal, and generous with the slate, he's the landlord we all dream of meeting.

3. THE JOCKEY
(SHAMELESS)

Like the *Star Wars* cantina re-imagined by Irvine Welsh, The Jockey (actually The Wellington in West Gorton) is prime example of Rough Pub local distinctiveness. Every day, the extended Maguire and Gallagher clans gather in front of the bar and go about their business. Regional goods are sold with minimal ecological footprint – i.e. everything is thieved from the local supermarket – while other perks include The Stone Roses on the jukebox, pills sold over the bar and saucy barmaid Karen. Although it's hardly the most salubrious boozer to have on your doorstep, you'd be hard pushed to knock what's on offer – and if you did, just remember the sage words of Jockey's most-vocal regular, Northern anti-hero Vernon Francis Gallagher (aka Frank): 'Stop whinging. Drink more!'

2. THE NAG'S HEAD
(ONLY FOOLS AND HORSES)

So integral to OFAH's success that it spawned its own board game – where

players compete to win drinks, take 'Del's Dares' and come a cropper if they sample 'Mike's Stew' – The Nag's Head retains a strong claim to be the perfect TV pub. Run by mild-mannered landlord Mike Fisher (Kenneth Macdonald, R.I.P) and staffed by a nefarious roll-call of regulars, it's a think-tank for Del Boy's more extravagant

ideas, in later series sparked by cocktails combining Crème de Menthe and Tizer. 'I've got so many of his slates under here I could re-tile me bloody roof!' exclaims Mike during one brainstorming session.

Central to a disastrous insurance claim in the episode 'Hole In One' when Albert contrives to fall through the cellar door, it's a boozy community centre where even the school reunion is held upstairs (remember there's-something-in-my-eye classic 'Class Of '62'?). And who could forget Rodney's crush on ditzy barmaid Nervous Nerys?

C'est magnifique, Hooky Street.

1. THE VIGILANTE
(CITIZEN SMITH)

Inspired by a drunken political activist who writer John Sullivan chanced upon in his local pub years before, late-1970s' sitcom Citizen Smith was at its best when urban guerrilla Wolfie (Robert Lindsay) was at his local watering hole and 'revolutionary nerve centre' The Vigilante.

Here the four-man membership of the Tooting Popular Front (sidekicks Speed, weedy pacifist Ken and hen-pecked waiter Tucker) gathered to hear the increasingly crazed schemes of their leader, a South London Che Guevara adrift in an age of punk.

For Wolfie, knowing where the next drink is coming from remains top priority. When he's not begging pints of best bitter from teetotal Ken ('It's made from hops; so it's really fruit juice') or girlfriend Shirley, he's grovelling to local Mr Big Harry Fenning for an extension on his slate until 'after the revolution'.

'Well, well, well, three-sixteenths of a second after opening time and Trotsky's already here,' says Fenning on discovering Wolfie at the bar. 'The only way I could keep you out of here is if I turned this pub into a job centre.'

For Wolfie, revenge always comes at closing time. 'One last fag then bop, bop, bop!' he fantasises, taking an imaginary machine gun to Fenning after a run-in over a disastrous TPF Sports night.

Wolfie might be daft, but he's not stupid. The inaugural 'Tooting Folk Festival' (where he performs 'Forward All Indian Men') leads to a triumphant victory against the local toffs, while a threat to jump off the pub roof turns out to be just a ruse to sell his memoirs.

'The iron man of Tooting has not been defeated!' he vows in final episode 'Sweet Sorrow', before sneaking out past the flowerbeds.

Farewell, Vigilante. ✠

THE PACK O'CARDS

HIGH STREET, COMBE MARTIN,
DEVON, EX34 0ET

A THING TO DO IN DEVON, WITH A DECK.

People do deranged things when faced with a pocketful of unexpected winnings. Viv Nicholson, the brassy, northern football pools winner, spent spent spent like crazy until she was declared bankrupt. 'King of the Chavs', Mikey Carroll, claims he pissed his way through his £8.5 million lottery win in three years (stopping only to bed 1,000 women and do countless wheel spins on the lawn of his mansion). It's nice to know that people have been this way throughout the ages, acting with a crazed determination when faced with a wad of cash they hadn't previously accounted for.

Devonian George Ley enjoyed a particularly big win on the cards back in 1690. In the flush of success, he declared he'd design a house based around the number systems in a set of cards. It would feature four floors (one for each suit), thirteen rooms (the number of cards per suit), fifty-two windows, fifty-two stairs and a ground area measuring (yes, you're probably way ahead of me here) fifty-two feet square. The resultant building, now a pub called, inevitably, The Pack O'Cards, looks less like the pristine pack your grandmother keeps for the odd hand of bridge and more like some kind of booze-fuelled ziggurat erected to the specifications of a pissed-up seventeenth-century Omar Sharif. Hats off and bottoms up to the Ley man and his perfect game – through one crazy moment, probably the early onset of dementia, he gave us one of the country's daftest-looking drinking holes. ✠

THE SWAN

86 WOOD STREET,
LIVERPOOL, L1 4DQ

**FOR THOSE ABOUT TO ROCK,
WE SALUTE YOU.**

If you think Korn comes in a packet, Green Day is an eco awareness initiative and The Tygers Of Pan Tang are an exotic exhibit at Knowsley Safari Park , the Swan probably isn't for you.

A rock Algonquin where arcane trivia is traded with the solemnity of state secrets and local legends drink 'til they drop (a plaque on the bar reads, cryptically 'Big Al fell here, 2001'), the only 'Wind Of Change' The Swan knows about was released by The Scorpions in 1991 (which, since you ask, was about the fall of the Berlin Wall).

Legendary in its grunginess, a reporter for the *Liverpool Echo* once commented of the (now refurbished) gents:

"I've yet to see anyone dare use the sit down facility for fear that a set of tentacles should curl up and haul them screaming down the pan."

But then what do you expect from a pub where Slash is all over the jukebox?

Molten Brown handwash and a bloke in the corner offering you aftershave?

Perfect after a long afternoon scouring the racks of nearby Hairy Records, this rock'n'roll Anfield even has papier mache arms protruding from the walls, greeting drinkers with fixed devil salutes. ✠

THE CORNUBIA

142 TEMPLE STREET, BRISTOL, BS1 6EN

BRISTOL'S BEST KEPT SECRET.

When trying to find a great boozer in Bristol, I asked a few reliable beer aficionados – i.e. my dad and his pisshead mates – where the best one was to be found. 'The Cornubia', they all said. 'It's Bristol's best-kept secret.' After forty-five minutes trying to find it, A to Z in hand, walking round in endless circles, five times past the Inland Revenue and the fire station, asking – nay begging – strangers for some kind of insider knowledge of their fair city, I can see how it came by that accolade.

By a cruel twist of fate and bad town planning, The Cornubia has ended up being almost totally hidden behind another building. Maybe this adds to the boozy allure. Like a CAMRA version of a Freemasons' lodge, maybe it's only easily accessible with a weird handshake and a sly wink. Thick irony is poured on when you realise that the pub is owned by the Hidden Brewery – their house special ale is called 'Hidden Pint'. If it hadn't have been for my Dad on the phone guiding me in like a Rough Pub air-traffic controller, I might very well have sacked it and buggered off home, that beer destined to remain a hidden pint for me forever. Great pub though – I just wish I could tell you how to get there. ⊹

THE RED LION

HIGH STREET, AVEBURY,
WILTSHIRE, SN8 1RF

WICCA'S WORLD: NEW MEANING FOR THE PHRASE DRINKING RITUAL.

It's not every day you get to buy King Arthur a pint. But roll up at The Red Lion during the solstice and chances are that you'll find Arthur – or at least, Arthur Uther Pendragon, a.k.a. 'The Real King Of England' – at the bar following a hard morning's Paganism at the nearby Standing Stones.

'This is the most Pagan pub in England,' he explains, nursing a pint of – what else? – Strongbow. 'It's a tribal gathering place, part of a tradition dating back to the Saxon Mead Hall and the Celtic Roundhouses.'

At midday, it's hard to reconcile a lunchtime menu including goat's cheese fritters with the debauched banquets of yore. But, by mid-afternoon, the American tourists have melted away and The Red Lion – a coaching inn dating to 1800 – takes on a more primal aspect. The scrumpy flows, guitars and drums appear, and the air is thick with talk of moon circles, earth goddesses and mysterious forces.

'People come here for one day and then find themselves returning over and over again,' explains Terry Dobney, pictured right, a.k.a. 'The Keeper of the Stones'. 'It's called the "elastic Avebury effect".'

A pub you're forced to revisit? We'll drink to that.

THE BRITISH OAK

77 GOOCH STREET NORTH,
SELLY OAK, BIRMINGHAM

IT'S THE CAT'S WHISKERS.

Set in a former industrial district of Birmingham that now resembles a demilitarised zone, Gooch Street is deserted, save for the national symbol of urban blight – a blue plastic bag flying from some wire-mesh fencing.

The side window is shattered. A sign on the door says: 'Strictly No Children Allowed'. An abandoned copy of the *Daily Sport* lies open on the table. The headline reads: 'Naughty Nicky likes to Strip To Status Quo'.

An NHS wheelchair gathers dust beneath a Birmingham City FC mirror. On the pool table, a cat lounges sleepily, daring anyone to disturb it. At the bar, it becomes clear that the pub has a back room. The sound of clinking glasses and raucous laughter suggest a wild party is slowly winding down.

'Is there another bar?'

The barman looks at me, non-committal. 'No.'

As he does, 'Hey Jude' blasts from the jukebox. As if on cue, the entire party sings along.

Periodically, cab drivers arrive. As revellers emerge bleary-eyed from the back room, they wear a glow that suggests they've gained immunity from the cares of the world. As he exits, one punter lights up. Has he heard of the smoking ban?

'Smoking ban?' he says, with a boozy grin. 'What fucking smoking ban?'

This is a great place to drink. ⌗

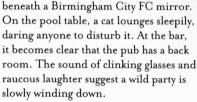

THE BRITISH OAK

'THE GOOD OLD DAYS'

WHEN DID IT BECOME OK TO TAKE CHILDREN INTO PUBS?

I don't remember when it became de rigueur to take kids into pubs. Once they were purely the playground of adults. Nowadays it seems compulsory to sit rocking a stroller back and forth from opening time 'til last orders while contemplating your fourth bottle of Aussie Chardonnay. How did this happen?

Back in the 1970s, I was intrigued – obsessed even – with what went on behind the closed doors of the public house. In fact, a worrying number of my childhood memories revolve around pubs in my native South Wales. Like so many kids of our generation, my brother and I would be left in the car outside the pub while whichever family members fancied a drink would sit inside, getting merry on the laughing water.

Happiness was a bottle of Coke, a packet of Chipmunk's Oxo flavour crisps and the radio tuned in as close to the Top 40 as we could get. Simon Bates would crackle in and out of the airwaves as the Welsh weather splashed the windscreen a muddy kind of clean. That time in the back seat of our clapped out Citroen Dyane instilled in me a healthy amount of patience. The inside of the pub was off limits, always – it might as well have had blue police tape wrapped round it and a yellow crime incident sign blocking the doorway. Kids just weren't welcome in that "speak when you're spoken to" world.

The problem nowadays is that such behaviour (i.e. leaving kids locked in the car outside the pub for three hours while you get smashed) would undoubtedly be labelled 'child abuse' by the PC police – the equivalent to leaving a dog in the back seat in the middle of summer. And we all know what happens then.

The closed shop policy was never more apparent than on one family holiday in the late '70s. Dad had planned to tour round Wales in a tent with myself and my brother in tow. We were joined by a few of my Dad's drinking buddies, the most notorious of them all being 'Uncle Klaus': a 6 foot 6 inch Estonian refugee in World War II who knew a thing or two about drinking beer.

The idea was that we would move from place to place, pitching the tent in the beer gardens of various pubs. If we were lucky, Dad would remember we were there and bring us rations of crisps and fizzy drinks every few hours until we fell asleep out of sheer boredom. Morning would invariably be broken with the sound of Uncle Klaus being sick inside his tent.

My perceptions of what a pub actually was were formed back here, from the outside looking in. I was convinced the pub was a wild place, untamed and unruly – like Ragnarok painted by Hogarth while he tripped out on scrumpy. All I knew was that I wanted in. I was constantly thinking "When I'm old enough, I'm going to live in the fucking pub…"

I still think of those times as the 'Good Old Days', back when the pub still retained some mystery. The problem nowadays is that parents want to have their cake and eat it too. They don't want to leave kids home alone (fair play, but it never did me any harm) and they also don't want to miss out on the action down the boozer. Surely one of the truly great things about the pub is that it's there to get away from screaming kids, to douse yourself in alcohol before going home and passing out?

The worst thing about it all is that kids hate the pub. They hate boozing, they hate the boredom it brings and they really hate the fact that mum and dad are uninterested in their every move and stink like a recycling bank. Parents just don't see it – either that or they choose to ignore it.

What I'm asking is "when does the fight back start"? I had to wait 'til I looked old enough to get served before I could revel in the smoky delights of the snug. Pubs are supposed to be for adults. They sell alcohol. People talk endless crap in them. That's the long and the short of it.

It's time to reclaim them from the evil forces of bad parenting.

Either that way or I'm going to have to take back the Scout hut by force.

'Dib Dib Dib' indeed. ✠

BRITON'S PROTECTION

50 GREAT BRIDGEWATER STREET, MANCHESTER, M1 5LE

UNKNOWN PLEASURES: MANCHESTER MUSIC MECCA.

One of the oldest pubs in central Manchester, the Briton's Protection has been at the heart of the city's music scene for as long as most people care to remember. Originally used as a recruiting post for troops for the Battle Of Waterloo, for anyone born in the latter half of the twentieth century, it is perhaps more significant for the fact that it is within spitting distance of the Haçienda (inexplicably knocked down and rebuilt as flats – even though they kept the name) and the offices of the legendary and much-missed manager of the Joy Division and New Order, Rob Gretton.

For years, the Briton's Protection acted as a secondary office for much of Rob's business. Dave Rofe, former Haçienda resident and manager of Doves, remembers how the bands and DJs associated with the club and labels used the 'BP' for 'all the "good" meetings, the ones that would extend into the night 'til beyond closing time, mental conversations about football, music, the Haç, whatever.' His favourite memory of the pub was: 'Rob standing in the backroom, arms outstretched, bellowing "City 'Til I Die" to a bunch of bemused office workers. It really was a constant for us, that place.'

With so little rock 'n' roll heritage left unmolested in the British Isles (see the bulldozering of The Cavern, The Marquee, The Haçienda – the list is endless), it's good to know that the Protection has hardly changed since it was Ian Curtis' local. ⳨

THE WELLINGTON ARMS

56 PARK ROAD, SOUTHAMPTON, HAMPSHIRE, SO15 3DE

PLANS FOR EMBASSY GO UP IN SMOKE.

Last year's smoking ban was an absurdly heavy-handed piece of legislation memorably described by David Hockney as 'destroying bohemia'. The only good things to emerge from it were the attempts by smokers to evade the ban by any means possible.

Like nicotine-driven officers in some boozy version of *The Great Escape*, their efforts ranged from the sublime to the ridiculous. In South Wales, property developer Kerry Morgan built his own private pub in the back garden. In Hereford, Tony Blows, licensee of the Dog Inn, simply carried on as though nothing had happened. In Halifax, an establishment called Mellor's Bar even renamed itself The Puff Inn. Most ingenious of all, though, was the scheme hatched by Bob Beech, landlord of The Wellington Arms in Southampton.

Like a modern-day Burgundy in *Passport to Pimlico*, Bob declared that the pub was the official embassy for Redonda, a tiny island lying 35 miles south west of Antigua. As such, it would technically be foreign soil, and, thanks to a legal loophole, outside the jurisdiction of the ban.

Assisted by Edward Elder – an old sailing pal of the island's king, and a long-term regular – Bob was duly knighted and hatched plans to serve alcohol at local prices. Seeing as Redonda is a one-mile square remnant of an extinct volcano in the Caribbean Sea, annexed by the British in 1865, these would have made even Wetherspoon's seem pricey. Sadly, Foreign Office red tape ensured the idea came to nothing, but Bob remains sanguine.

'It was a good plan and we got some publicity out of it, but what can you do?' he laughs. 'We've got a nice outdoor area for smokers now and we're still the official consulate of the Kingdom Of Redonda.'

THE HORSE SHOE

17-19 DRURY STREET,
GLASGOW, G2 5AE

THE LONGEST BAR IN THE UK.

It's difficult writing about The Horse Shoe without mentioning the fact that inexplicably huge indie milksops Travis used to rehearse upstairs, but we'll give it a damn good go. Ornate and beautifully preserved, The Horse Shoe is one of the last few untouched 'gin palace pubs' of the early twentieth century, one of those amazing architectural time-warps that immediately sends you back to a time of horse-drawn carriages, cholera and Jack the Ripper (OK, geographically wrong – maybe he was on a short city break). Featuring the longest continuous bar in the UK, The Horse Shoe can also proudly state that it was one of the last boozers on the mainland where Ollie Reed would rock up before flying to Malta to film *Gladiator*. We all know what happened next.

Sadly no longer offering the three-course lunch for one pound that used to be a staple for bands and students back in the 1980s, The Horse Shoe remains at the heart of Glasgow city life, packing them in night after night with some of the best, modestly priced ale in town. Keen observers of rock history should look out for the glass case on the wall, where a clutch of awards for Travis, the band who used... oh bollocks. There, I've just gone and done it. ⌗

No. 32

THE THREE LEGS

THE HEADROW, LEEDS,
WEST YORKSHIRE, LS1 6PU

**FOR WHEN YOU WANT TO GO OUT ON A
LIMB...**

Leeds city centre: a glittering metropolis
of Victorian arcades and steel'n'glass
where you can hardly hear yourself think
above the clatter of Manolos en route to
Harvey Nick's.

And then there's The Three Legs. Pass
through these portico doors and you'll
return to a less-sanitised age, where a pint
meant Double Diamond, Don Revie was
God and Caramel Macchiato could be
a tricky opponent for Big Daddy on the
Saturday afternoon wrestling card.

On the tables, beer mats recommend
'Tia Maria – a drink for every occasion'. At
the bar, an all-ages clientele work on their
drinking like golfers on their handicap
and attention rarely strays from the racing
beamed on the overhead television. The
overall effect is so evocative of a bygone

era you half expect Ted Heath to interrupt
the five o'clock from Leopardstown to
announce a power cut.

'I've been coming here for thirty years,'
says a regular called Peter, dapper in a
stove-pipe hat. 'It's a rough-and-ready
pub, no frills. The only thing that's
changed is that someone painted the
bloody walls orange.'

The Three Legs: this one will run and
run. ⌖

THE WELL HOUSE TAVERN

CATHEDRAL YARD, EXETER,
EX1 1HD

SKELETON STAFF: AND THEY MAKE NO BONES ABOUT IT…

It's always comforting to know that someone in the pub is in a worse state than you. Midday on a Monday in The Well House Tavern, opposite the cathedral in the centre of sleepy Exeter, there are the usual set of reliable old soaks, already deep in conversation about everything from nearby brewery taps and local beer festivals to Hughie Green and the (alleged) bizarre drugs-and-wanking-based death of Michael Hutchence.

Amazingly, these guys, nursing their career hangovers, have nothing on the dude in the basement. Encased in glass in a musty cellar is a set of bones belonging to someone who died of the Black Death on this site. No matter how bad the hangover is, at least those guys upstairs were going to drink their way back to some kind of skewed sense (via the unarguably brilliant selection of locally sourced ales). The poor bugger in the glass case, however, can't even get excavated out of the place by the Natural History Museum. Next time you're in the area, this place is a must, as long as you remember to buy one for our incapacitated friend downstairs. It's the least you can do to pay tribute and raise a glass to them dry old bones. ☩

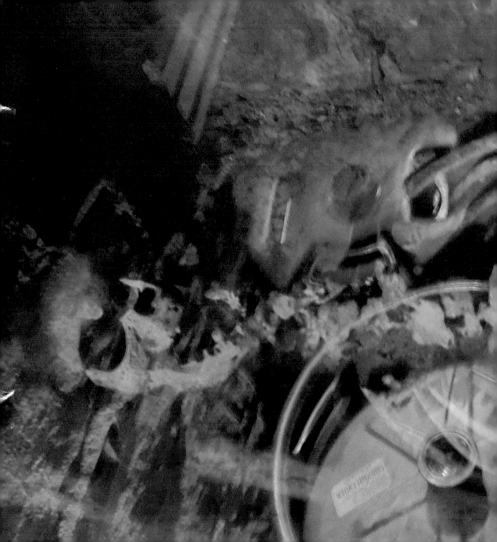

'LIGHTS CAMRA ACTION!'

THE PUB IN BRITISH CINEMA

First, the good news. A vast array of classic pub interiors have been saved from the developers' wrecking ball forever. Within these smoky, dark-wood interiors you'll find enough dubious characters, flirtatious barmaids and drunken wits to light up Blackpool illuminations, Plymouth Hoe and the Oxford Street Christmas lights. The bad news? They only exist on celluloid.

British cinema has long used the pub as a handy parallel for the world at large. In the classic 1942 propaganda flick *The Day Will Dawn*, a harrowing description of hearing Hitler laugh unites the pub – and, by proxy, the nation – as the country teeters on the brink of war. In 1949's *Passport to Pimlico* – where the locals discover that, technically, they're free from post-war privations – it's in their local pub that they tear up their ration books and opt for a decadent life free from responsibility (a rare case of the revolution actually starting at closing time).

By the fifties, the demand for dewy-eyed barmaids and square-jawed heroes gasping for an Ice Cold In Alex was on the wane. Filmed in Coronation Year, 1953's *Time Bomb* and classic Ealing comedy *The Titfield Thunderbolt* saw the pub reverting to its natural role as the centre of the community, where traditional values triumph in the face of adversity. It was only with the arrival of the angry young men that the pub was restored to centre stage. In *Saturday Night And Sunday Morning*, Arthur Seaton (Albert Finney) is a hard-drinking anti-hero who falls down the stairs of his local after a drinking contest and still manages to up-end girlfriend Brenda the same night. 'What I'm out for is a good time. Everything else is propaganda,' he rants, inspiring everyone from Morrissey to the Arctic Monkeys in the process.

For Arthur the pub is a refuge, a boss-free zone where class pride swells with every drink. "Don't let the bastards grind you down that's one thing I've learned" he says, hand on the lathe, mind on a pint at The White Horse. "I'd like to see anybody

try and grind me down, that'd be the day."

If *Room At The Top* and *This Sporting Life* both boast gratifyingly pivotal pub scenes, it's 1962's *Saturday Night* which provides the richest pickings. It might lack a similarly punchy social agenda, but the scene where The Searchers play to a pub heaving with chain-smoking drinkers says more about this bygone age than any amount of furrowed brow proselytising (proof, perhaps, that it's often the films that don't try to tell us anything that say the most).

By the mid-sixties, the pub, much like the nation, had regained its sense of fun. In *Help!* Ringo's enjoyment of a lager 'n' lime is pre-empted when he exits The Turk's Head in Twickenham – in film world, a short dash from Buck House – through a pub trap door. In *Up The Junction*, much needed light relief is supplied when a kohl-eyed Maureen Lipman leads the locals through a psychedelic sing-song. Trawl through the archives and you'll find innumerable examples of this curious collision of old 'n' new: long-haired boys in butterfly collars and girls in Mary Quant dresses nursing dimpled pint pots and smoking B&H.

By the start of the seventies, a new, more

In *Get Carter*, Newcastle is portrayed as a claustrophobic maze of terraced streets where Jack Carter's (Michael Caine, of course) visit to The Vick and Comet brings him face to face with the world he left behind. When he asks for a pint of bitter in "a thin glass", you can almost hear the crack as the North-South divide goes from hairline fracture to tectonic shift. In Stanley Kubrick's *Clockwork Orange*, the Korova Milk Bar might not look much like a conventional pub, but its notion of the pub as a fermentation tank for violence still haunts the *Daily Mail* to this day.

Pubs might have been seedy, smoky and violent in the 1970s, but they had their upside, too. Mick Travis' trip into a pub back room in *O Lucky Man!* can still raise temperatures, while The Green Man pub

malevolent spirit was in the air. No longer would the lounge bars of the nation be a playground for bright young things to frolic after a hard day's grooving. Like the decade they mirrored, pubs would become sexy and dangerous all at once.

in *The Wicker Man* (The Ellangowan Hotel – see pp.126-127) regularly fields visitors with a soft spot for Britt Ekland (right). Impossible, too, not to mention John Landis' honorary Brit-flick *American Werewolf In London*, where the locals at the Slaughtered Lamb – including a young Rik Mayall – provide an uncanny representation of rural hospitality.

By the eighties, the old ways were going up in smoke (literally, in the case of *The Long Good Friday*'s Lion And Unicorn, blown up by the IRA). With the nation divided between, in TV comedy terms, supporters of Loadsamoney and Yosser Hughes, it took a maverick genius like Bruce Robinson to realise that a better future might come from re-examining the past.

Withnail And I is, as film-buffs' essential *Your Face Here* declared, 'one of the best-loved comedies of all time', but its pub scenes achieve the near impossible feat of being universally feted and, even now, laugh-out loud funny. For the shell-shocked duo, the pub is a handy bunker

in which to shelter from the bombardment of horrors offered by the real world. Looking back, it's hard not to see Withnail as a contributory factor in the rise of Britpop, a tipping point where the past was seen as a good thing per se – and every pop star dreamed of acting like Withnail and looking like Marwood.

Little wonder that few on-screen pubs have matched up since. *Trainspotting* might have provided a harrowingly accurate portrayal of Leith's lunatic pub fringe, but no one ever dreamed of sharing a pint with Begbie. Guy Ritchie's *Lock Stock and Two Smoking Barrels* struggled hard for cult status with its retro swagger and boozy pow-wows at Samaon Joe's but still ended up a bit of a two and eight. It says much about the current climate that the most famous pub of recent years was The Winchester in *Shaun of the Dead* – a derelict hovel frequented by zombies.

Visiting some of these pubs today is a sobering experience. The Vick and Comet is now a branch of Bakers Oven (cue irate pub fans quoting the line: 'The only reason I came back to this crap house is to find out who did it' to bewildered shop girls). The Old Mother Black Cap, where Withnail orders 'Two large gins, two pints of cider, ice in the cider', is now a gastro-pub called The Tavistock Arms.

In May 2008, I took a trip to South East London to check out the Albany Arms (right), the pub used in the final scenes of *Shaun of the Dead*. On arrival I found it boarded up and derelict, surrounded by men in hard hats

preparing to put it out of its misery.

What, I wonder, would Arthur Seaton – a stickler for the old ways – make of such cultural vandalism? Would Withnail, drunk and raving, react with the words: 'What fucker's done that?'

We'd like to think so. Still, if the glory days of pub cinema are over, raising a toast to these boozy palaces of the big screen seems a fitting place to finish.

Fade to black. Roll credits.

The end. ✠

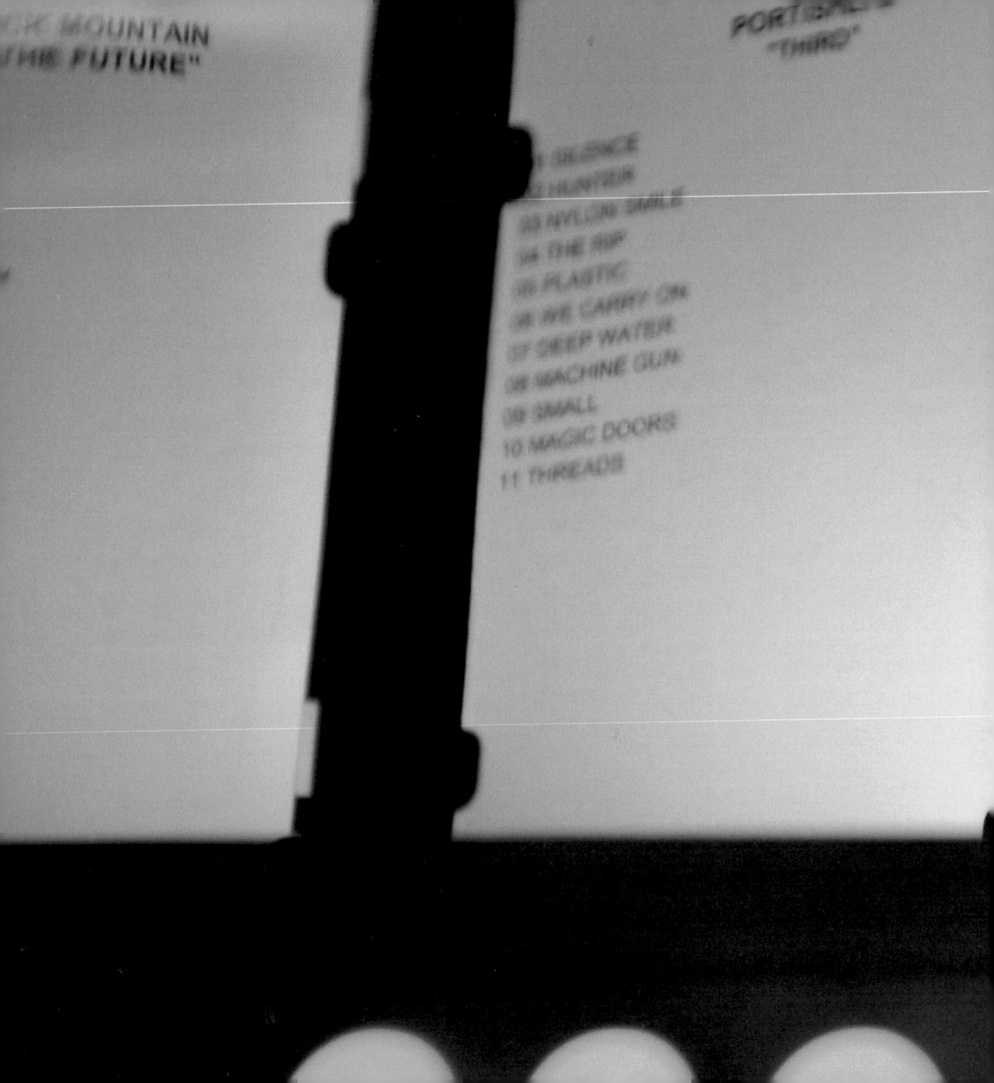

BLACK MOUNTAIN
"THE FUTURE"

01 SILENCE
02 HUNTER
03 NYLON SMILE
04 THE RIP
05 PLASTIC
06 WE CARRY ON
07 DEEP WATER
08 MACHINE GUN
09 SMALL
10 MAGIC DOORS
11 THREADS

ROUGH PUBS
30 TO 21

30 THE CHARLIE CHAPLIN
29 THE LAMP TAVERN
28 HALFWAY HOUSE
27 ELI'S (ROSE AND CROWN)
26 THE NUTSHELL
25 THE PLOUGH AND HARROW
24 THE INTREPID FOX
23 THE COACH AND HORSES
22 THE SAIR INN
21 THE WINDSOR CASTLE

01 RO
02 WA
03 SE
04 SL
05 SR
06 HA
07 ME
08 DE
09 SC
10 DIS

No. 30

THE CHARLIE CHAPLIN

26 New Kent Rd, Elephant and Castle, London, SE1 6TJ

COMES WITH ADDED COMEDY VALUE.

'One of the capital's biggest monstrosities, worthy only of the demolition ball,' read the thoughts of one dissatisfied customer on a pro-pubs website.

'Gives you the impression you've been sectioned,' reads another.

With friends like this, who needs enemies?

Squeezed between the Coronet cinema and the pink pleasure dome of the Elephant and Castle shopping centre, The Chaplin won't be turning up on Grand Designs any time soon. Unless, that is, Siberian gulag chic storms the broadsheets, and Trinny and Susannah are pictured quaffing Fosters Ice on the terrace, swathed in ironic Burberry.

Inside, a motley collection of drunks, dipsos and the generally merry engage in the sort of apple 'n' pears patter Guy Ritchie dreams about.

'They bottled it as soon as they clocked me' says one bloke more wired than BT.

'I'm just back from Thailand. Did four years. It would have been fifteen, but I got a royal pardon,' says another.

'Anyone fancy a Southern Comfort?' says the barmaid, waving a generously filled glass aloft.

Can you ever have too much Charlie? Not here. A ten-foot effigy on the wall outside lures in thirsty punters, while framed photos remind drinkers that our hero started his journey to the silver screen from nearby East Street.

Plans are afoot to flatten the entire area in 2010 and replace it with (yes) a shopping mall. The pictures of Charlie will end up in a dustcart and locals will be forced to drink frappuccino.

Visit while you still can. ✢

THE LAMP TAVERN

257 BARFORD STREET, BIRMINGHAM,
WEST MIDLANDS, B5 6AH

**THERE IS A LIGHT THAT NEVER
GOES OUT.**

In 1871, at Birmingham's boozy peak, there were ten pubs on Barford Street. As a result of The Duke Of Wellington's 1830 Beerhouse Act – which allowed pubs to open for eighteen hours a day – thirsty factory workers would descend on the area to enjoy a pint of their favoured tipple: 'a sweet dark mild'.

The Army & Navy, The Coventry Arms, The Goffs Arms, The Nelson and The Hand and Bottle have long gone. In more recent times, The Malt and Shovel, The Vulcan and The Roebuck have also slithered down the plughole of history. Today, only The Lamp remains, a small beacon of hope amid the dark clouds of 'progress'. Inside, little has changed since the *Birmingham Daily Mail* described it in 1834 as 'a simple dark room with basic furniture'.

Behind the counter, the menu stretches from pickled mussels to pork scratchings. The beer is great, too; it's the only pub in Birmingham serving Stanway Stanney Bitter, the award-winning Cotswolds ale.

No wonder The Lamp inspires such fierce loyalty. The men of the Jockey Morris club drink here after rehersals, while a 5 a.m. license means that landlord Eddie Fitzpatrick more often than not sees in the dawn chatting with regulars. ⸸

HALFWAY HOUSE

24 FLESHMARKET CLOSE,
EDINBURGH, SCOTLAND

UPTOWN TOP RANKIN.

A boozy Hobbit Hole crouched near the entrance to Edinburgh Station, the Halfway House has a strong claim to being the nation's most handily placed railway pub. Arrive here a quarter of an hour before your train leaves, and you'll have time to throw back a couple of pints, moan about the weather and tour the premises before the guard parps his whistle. Not that the tour would take very long. The Halfway is so small that even Bilbo Baggins would consider it cramped.

Originally a bolt-hole for blood-stained workers from the nearby slaughterhouse, business soared when an umbrella factory opened next door. These days, tourists are lured in by a Sassenach-baffling menu including haggis, neeps and tatties, but delve into the cupboards and you'll hear the rattle of bones.

Victorian rogue – and inspiration for *Dr Jekyll and Mr Hyde* – Deacon Brodie drank here, while Ian Rankin's Dr Rebus uncovered skeletons in a pub on this spot in the book *Fleshmarket Close*. ✠

ELI'S
(A.K.A. THE ROSE & CROWN)

HUISH EPISCOPI, SOMERSET, TA10 9QT

PRIDE OF THE WILD WEST COUNTRY.

In Ian Marchant's travelogue-cum-boozer's bible *The Longest Crawl*, he is directed again and again by misty-eyed converts towards a West Country pub called Eli's. One of the last unspoilt pubs in the UK, Eli's (actually called the Rose & Crown, but nicknamed after the father of the current landlady) has fantastically avoided the dread hand of progress. Set in a picture-perfect village and advertising the imminent arrival of Morris Men, Eli's timewarps you back into a beatific, pre-Second World War world that's far more cream teas, cricket whites and warm beer than micro-keg lager, hoodies and Kalamata olives.

The bar lies somewhere inside the rabbit warren of small rooms, dusty and silent with history and looking like they've just been dusted off for the first time since the 1940s. Ostensibly just an open room, it gives the impression that you're stood there serving with the landlord. Tucked away inconspicuously at the far end is surely one of the greatest inventions of the twentieth century, the Dalex Beer Engine. Far more useful than the A bomb or sliced bread, the Beer Engine is a vertical double pump that enables the delivery of two smooth pots of foaming nut-brown ale without too much arm-wrestling effort from the bar staff – the lazy man's short cut to a perfect pint. Preserved beautifully in well-worn wood, the Beer Engine, like Eli's itself, is conclusive proof that the old ways really were the best. ✠

THE NUTSHELL

THE TRAVERSE, BURY ST EDMUNDS, SUFFOLK, IP33 1BJ

SMALL BEER: TINIEST PUB IN THE BRITISH ISLES.

The title of smallest pub in Britain is highly contested. Venues in Dorset, Merseyside, Kent and Brighton proudly state that they are in fact the tiniest in the land, seemingly unaware that, if it was true, there would be no way that they could cope with the influx of extra trade they might see from curious day-tripping boozers. That aside, there is only room for one of them in the *Guinness Book of Records* and Norris McWhirter's approval is proof enough for us. Plus there are enough eccentric touches in this place to warrant an entry here, so let's kill two birds with one stone.

The Nutshell in Bury St Edmunds measures a claustrophobic 5m by 2m. There are two tables, each with seating for two or three people. And the moment you start thinking about the possibilities of swinging a cat, you notice somebody thought of it

before you – there is a mummified moggy hanging from the ceiling (alongside a couple of calcified rodents). The ceiling is plastered with defaced foreign bank notes; the walls are dotted with coins from all around the world.

Everything else in the pub vies for room and there really isn't that much to spare. The jar of pickled eggs on the bar is so ludicrously oversized, it seems like a prop from *Land of the Giants*. A bag of scampi fries placed on the bar assumes the proportions of the weekly shopping from Tesco. The effect is dizzying. In fact, it's enough to drive you to drink.

On buying my third pint, I decide to enquire about the blackened corpse of the former feline dangling over the bar.

'It's to help ward off any evil spirits,' says the barman.

'Does it work?'

Without missing a beat, he replies, 'Well, we don't stock Campari.' ✠

REBELLIOUS JUKEBOX

PUTTING ON THE STYLUS: AN APPRECIATION OF THE PUB JUKEBOX.

I t is always reassuringly the same. First the slam-dunk thunk as the coin falls home. Then the machine shakes itself alive, whirr – click – whirr as the well-worn piece of PVC, just seven inches in diameter with an inch or so of the centre dinked out, is moved upright into a gravity-defying position, revolving at a steady forty-five revolutions per minute. The first, tentative crackles as the needle hits its groove are all anticipation, like the precious last few time-stretched seconds before an aeroplane touches down. Finally, a burst of sound as the song starts, like jet engines, like the sonic boom. This is rock 'n' roll made more aggressive after

being compressed through the machine's one speaker (let's face it, this machine was built solely for rock 'n' roll – and, more's the point, for ugly three-minute primal screams). This, after all, is a machine that is always punk rock, never prog, never acid house. As the last chords fade, the machine patiently and lovingly returns the record to its rightful place and starts the process again. Without trying to get too Nick Hornby on the matter, there really is nothing better than pumping coins into a well-stocked pub jukebox.

The classic jukebox, the one made with chrome and moulded plastic, the one with a name like Wurlitzer or Rock-Ola

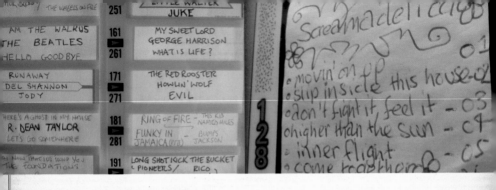

or Continental, has now all but been replaced in the corner of the lounge bar of your local. Just as vinyl was read the last rites by the compact disc, the 7" jukebox gave way to its CD cousin, the more boring, more 'practical' version. In terms of storage, vinyl players could hold a maximum of 200 sides of vinyl whereas the standard CD jukebox could hold 100 albums with tracks of any length. As the jukebox randomises, you start to hear odder and odder music, as the sorry depths of the last few tracks on side two of an album are broadcast to the public for the first time. Another consequence of CD technology is that anything goes now. No longer is it the last refuge for gonzo-skronk rock classics like 'Blockbuster' by The Sweet or 'Ace Of Spades', 'Another

Girl, Another Planet' or 'School's Out' – now everything from 'Bat Out Of Hell' to 'I Am The Resurrection' becomes musical fair game before closing time. Nine minutes fifty seconds must seem like value for money when you're down to your last 20p and the 'time please' bell has been struck.

Maybe the next stage of pointless reinvention is the MP3 jukebox – surely the least sexy prospect yet – that will allow a punter to choose from every record the bloke behind the bar has ever bought. Personally, I find it pretty much impossible to imagine Joan Jett declaring her love of rock 'n' roll perched next to a glorified iPod. Until that inevitable day, here are some images from our favourite jukeboxes in the UK. ✠

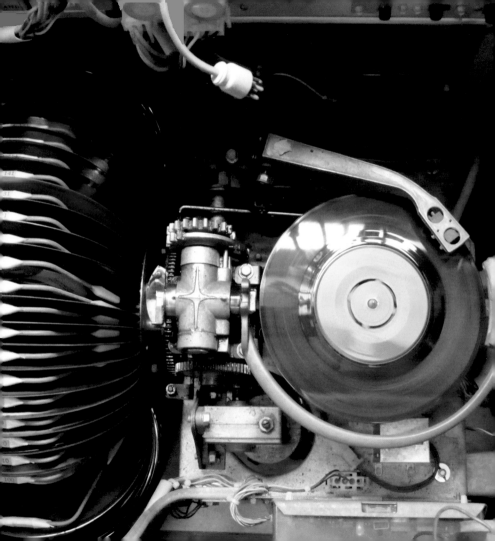

No. 25
THE PLOUGH AND HARROW

MONKNASH, NR COWBRIDGE,
GLAMORGAN, CF71 7QQ

WELSH DRINKERS TAKE THEIR LEAKS OUTSIDE.

It might not be every day that Wales win the Grand Slam, but it's good to know that that when they do, you can watch the match on a giant screen in front of a roaring log fire in a picture-perfect pub. Set in rolling bucolic countryside deep in the land of my fathers, The Plough is a national treasure that has played host to local heroes like Gavin Henson and James Dean Bradfield.

Situated a short walk from the kind of secluded coastline that would make Nicholas Crane fall to his knees

and weep with unbridled joy, a few years ago, the Wales Tourist Board chose the idyllic Plough And Harrow to represent all that is great and good about the Principality in a single image. It has also been awarded CAMRA's Welsh Pub of the Year award five times. This despite the fact that the gents is outside, meaning that in typical Welsh weather you have no choice but to get absolutely soaked whenever you need to slash. Still, who gives a toss when there's a glowing hearth, six real ales on gravity and home-made faggots for sale?

Iechyd da, butty! Bottoms up!

THE INTREPID FOX

15 GILES STREET, LONDON, WC2H 8LN

TOUCHED BY THE HAND OF GOTH.

A decade or so ago, I used to work opposite The Intrepid Fox in Soho. Although it was central London's premier metallers' hangout, I used to drink in there occasionally, mainly because the quiz machine they had seemed to pay out more often than all the others in the area. One summer's day, I walked into the office and witnessed a team of Bible-black clad Goths hoisting a gigantic gargoyle above the door. That was the Fox – determinedly – nay, dementedly – different to everything else around. Their idea of a refit was slapping the current Alien Sex Fiend tour poster over the previous year's one; their idea of a cocktail hour was shotgunning Snakebite and Black at midnight. Far more Aleister Crowley than Alastair Sawday, and thank God for that.

Progress, though, did come up and bite The Fox in the neck. Acquired for redevelopment in 2006 it was cruelly boarded up in preparation for housing a few moneyed ponsonbys who could fruit about the West End bragging into their iPhones. Needless to say, work has yet to begin.

On a happier note, there were stirrings in the West End in the dead of night. Like all good denizens of the underworld, The Intrepid Fox just wouldn't stay dead. Relocating to an even grungier locale in the shadow of Centrepoint, The Fox was reborn, Phoenix-like. Now crazier than ever, The Fox remains the one-stop destination for London's unreconstructed rock 'n' rollers. Here, Kurt Cobain will never die and music might as well have stopped with the guitar solo from 'Sweet Child Of Mine'. The Intrepid Fox – conclusive proof that not only does the Devil have the best tunes, he can keep a damn good pint of Strongbow, too… ☩

THE COACH & HORSES

29 GREEK STREET,
LONDON, W1V 5LL

HANGOVER SQUARE: SOHO LITERARY INSTITUTION.

Although many pubs in Soho can stake a claim to having helped all manner of legendary drinkers on their voyage to the grave (Francis Bacon swapping paintings for alcohol at the Colony Rooms; Dylan Thomas losing the only manuscript for 'Under Milk Wood' in the Admiral Duncan – the list is endless), only The Coach & Horses has continually basked in its reputation as a filling station for London's greatest artistic drunks.

Under the patronage of 'London's rudest landlord', Norman Balon, it served just about passable beer and absolutely no good cheer whatsoever. But customers like Peter Cook and Peter O'Toole liked it just that way – no bullshit, just meat-and-potatoes boozing. *Private Eye* magazine held their editorials in the upstairs room, while

Keith Waterhouse's play, 'Jeffrey Bernard Is Unwell', is ostensibly a monologue that finds the infamous *Spectator* hack locked in The Coach. All in all, tough competition for today's Soho drinker.

A minor makeover since Balon's recent retirement was of the very best kind. The 1950s' interior was left pretty much untouched, the toilets were cleaned (possibly for the first time ever) and the beer was brought up to scratch with the rest of the pubs in the area. Thankfully, though, the last fifty years of Soho history still positively haunt this place. The photos on the walls act as a permanent tribute to the greats and the spirits of those legends remain, propping up the bar, griping away about tourists and the price of booze until chucking out time comes around and they stagger home to the great snug bar in the sky. Really, who'd want them any other way?

LUNCH

THE SAIR INN

139 LANE TOP, LINTHWAITE,
YORKSHIRE, HD7 5SG

PEAKS AND TROUGHS...

Situated at the top of a steep hill along the A62 to Oldham, the Sair Inn isn't much to look at. The pub sign – a drunken pig – is the sort of thing that makes computer graphics seem like a good idea, while if you show up before 5pm you'll find the door firmly closed. Gain entry, however, and you'll discover open fires in every room, rough flagstone floors and a chintz-free ambience presided over by legendary landlord Ron Crabtree.

On the jukebox, five tracks for a quid gets you access to a seam of the musical goldmine stretching from Sonny Boy Williamson to Cream. In the back room, a selection of board games are available for those loath to take on the locals at shove ha'penny, while behind the bar a sign reads: 'We Serve Drinks, Not Drunks – Ron Excepted'.

A worthy winner of CAMRA's Pub of the Year in 1997, The Sair continues to attract beer connoisseurs thanks to own-brewed ales including Autumn Gold and the deadly Leadboiler. But a visit here is about more than hops and barley. In this boozy Bermuda triangle, hours vanish like sea-tossed yachts on radar, and a sense of wellbeing grows with every trip to the bar.

'That's the thing about coming to this pub,' grins Ron, gazing out through the window at the Colne Valley below. 'It's all downhill from here.' ✛

THE WINDSOR CASTLE

27–29 CRAWFORD MEWS, MARBLE ARCH, LONDON W1H 4LQ

SOMETHING WHISKERED THIS WAY COMES.

'Oliver Reed was a good customer,' says landlord Michael Tierney, adjusting his monocle. 'And Richard Harris was a regular too, when he was living at The Savoy.'

Such is the wonder of The Windsor Castle. More like the mythical English pubs seen on the soundstages of Hollywood than a bar tucked away behind the roar of the Edgware Road, it's as camp as Christmas and twice as much fun.

Outside the front door, a model soldier stands to attention in a full-sized sentry box. On the walls, generations of royalty jockey for position like crowds at Balmoral. Above the bar, snapshots of English sporting heroes rub shoulders with the alcoholic elite of the showbiz set, and a saturnine George Best catches the eye.

It's a cosy, cliquey kind of place with a rosy glow and copper-top tables, where you half expect to see the Major from Fawlty Towers downing a Drambuie.

Prominent among the regulars are The Handlebar Club. Arrive during one of their monthly meetings and you'll hear talk of everything from briar-smoking to baling twine, with Bombardier the drink of choice.

I fall into conversation with a man in a blazer and tie, sporting a Dick Dastardly moustache. We lament the decline of the English pub.

'I know where all the old pubs are going,' he says cryptically, his bristles twitching. 'It's the damned Americans. They're taking our pubs and rebuilding them brick by brick in Texas.' ✠

DARTS OF PLEASURE

SLINGS, ARROWS AND OUTRAGEOUS FORTUNE: A SHORT HISTORY OF PUB SPORTS.

There's nothing like a well-balanced pub game; it's a healthy mixture of sporting rivalry, who-cares fun and friendly combat too rarely experienced in these paranoid times.

Where did this mania for booze-related competition come from?

The Romans, inevitably. Ever since the introduction of chequers at the local taberna, the British pub game has adapted with the times, often incurring the wrath of the authorities along the way.

As long ago as 1495, Henry VII passed a statute restricting 'the indoor games that are distracting Tudor pubmen from archery', and that was before they'd invented darts. The Elizabethans' love of quoits – a game traditionally played by miners – was seen as being so unhealthy that there were efforts to ban it, while the craze for skittles in the seventeenth century still echoes around every local bowling alley.

Sadly, reckless pursuits like 'Conga Cuddling' – where human skittles are knocked down by an eel swung on a rope – are behind us, but strange practices continue. 'Dwyle Flunking' – a tug o' war over a sodden beer towel – is still practised at The Lewes Arms (pages 152–153), while 'Rhubarb Thrashing' – where two blindfolded opponents flay each other with a root vegetable – is a feature of gigs by West Country prog-rockers Stackridge.

Reduce any of these activities in a petri-dish and the same basic formula emerges: the pub game is an excuse to pit your wits against an opponent, place a bet, and assert a little local pride.

Of the modern pub staples, darts was only popularised when George VI casually threw an arrow while visiting a social club in Slough in 1937. The growth of US import pocket billiards – universally known as 'pool' – in the 1970s and '80s (in 1960 there wasn't a single table in the UK, now there are over 50,000) seemed to owe as much to student lifestyles as to low running costs.

It is a real shame then that these pursuits are dying out as we become more and more insular, glued to our computers and loath to leave our front rooms. Today traditional games like Aunt Sally, Pitch Penny and Shuffleboard, are all but extinct, wiped out by battalions of high-tech quiz games, Xbox 360s and merciless one-arm bandits. Our darts players, meanwhile, are being washed away on a tide of sea bass, victims of gastro re-furbs where the oche is the first thing to go.

Next time you're in the local, throw some arrows. Let's save our (pub) sports. ✠

LAMB

IMPORTED

EST.

Genuine

NAVY R

Produce of

700 ml e

A smooth and mellow quality rum from
ALFRED LAMB INTERNATIONAL LIMITED, LONDON

ROUGH PUB

20 - 11

20 - THE FLYING SCOTSMAN

19 - THE PALM TREE

18 - THE TINNERS ARMS

17 - THE YEW TREE

16 - THE HEART & HAND

15 - THE FREE TRADE INN

14 - THE ACE OF SPADES

13 - THE GREEN MAN

12 - THE ELLANGOWAN

11 - THE PILCHARD INN

700 ML

E
**OUS
USE**
RESERVE

CH WHISKY

YEARS

700ml

SCOTLAND

THE FLYING SCOTSMAN

2–4 CALEDONIAN ROAD,
LONDON, N1 9DU

SEX AND THE CITY: LEGENDARY LONDON STRIP PUB.

Two hundred yards from the gleaming flutes of the St Pancras Champagne Bar lurks an altogether seedier drinking experience. A defiant two fingers up to the gentrification going on around it, The Scotsman is a strip pub and proud of it, a throwback to the days when The Scala was an all-night cinema, the Gattopardo coffee bar was booming and nightfall would see nylon-shirted businessmen drop by en route to the private film clubs of Pentonville Road.

Not for The Scotsman a Spearmint Rhino-style makeover as affected by its South London rival The Queen Anne. At this blacked-out bunker of sleaze they like to do things the old-fashioned way. Reputedly the last pub in London to have had a sawdust floor, here the windows are boarded up, eye contact is kept to a sex shop minimum, and

when we visit, even the pub sign had disappeared.

On the wall, a chalkboard with the words 'Dishes of the Day' lists a roll-call of dancers (Sindy, Camilla, Krystal). On the makeshift stage, girls gyrate listlessly to backing tapes as though in an endless audition for 'Readers' Wives' – The Musical'.

As each girl performs, another wafts through in a negligee, waving a pint pot full of change under the nose of punters (fifty pence is the going rate, but big tippers are remembered come show time). Bar staff take their cue from a sticker on the (empty) sandwich counter that reads 'Shit Happens'. The toilets – rumoured to be the inspiration for the Dante-esque khazi Ewan McGregor descended into in *Trainspotting* – don't appear to have been cleaned this century.

If the walls could talk, they'd have closed The Scotsman down years ago.

See you at the bar. ✠

THE PALM TREE

HAVERFIELD ROAD, BOW,
LONDON, E3 5BH

BOW SELECTER.

Stuck out on the edge of the Regent's Canal, The Palm Tree is blissfully out of step with the rest of London. Looking like it's been dropped fully formed into a waterside wilderness, the only thing left standing in a bomb-damaged street, the pub deftly manages to walk the tightrope between being a proper locals' boozer and a hangout for the East End's bright-eyed hip young things. Here, the beautiful people rub shoulders with Walford's finest in a pub that is determinedly old school (possibly why it gets nods from CAMRA). Behind the bar there are unchilled bottled beers (clearly the mindset is that if anyone is daft enough to drink them he deserves a warm beer). Gold and black wallpaper covers the place, treading a fine line between eyesore tack and Conran Shop finery. Then there's the entertainment.

On a frantic Saturday night, there's live music and it's just about standing room only. Crowds crush to get to the bar while a band, fronted by a fantastic end-of-the-pier Dean Martin-alike, fire up 'lounge lizard' standards with a constantly changing set of singers. What could be embarrassing karaoke turns by slightly worse-for-wear locals ends up feeling more like Vegas by way of sunny Hackney – the fat dancer from Take That could learn a thing or two about showmanship in here. An ageing couple gracefully dancing across the crowded barroom floor is pure Martin Parr.

Looking around, it dawns on you that everyone in the place is beaming from ear to ear. The next thing you realise is that it's one in the morning, you're happily plastered and you're contemplating swimming down to the nearest lock in order to get home. Come here and swing while you're swilling at one of the East End's finest boozers.

THE TINNERS ARMS

NOT FOR THE ZENNOR-PHOBIC.

They like to do things the old-fashioned way at The Tinners Arms. A stone structure built in 1271 to accommodate masons working on the nearby St Senara's Church, it's the sort of pub where they can still remember shaking their heads with dismay the day they opened the old school.

Situated five miles from St Ives, it's a handy pit-stop for walkers on the coastal path seeking refreshment after a hard morning marvelling over the local scenery.

'At Zennor one sees infinite Atlantic, all peacock-mingled colours, and the gorse is sunshine itself. It is the best place I have been,' enthused D.H. Lawrence in 1916.

That's as maybe, but don't expect to be treated like a long-lost brother at the Tinners. London ways are frowned upon along this jagged outcrop of coastland, and the proliferation of black Cornish flags is a reminder that visitors from across the Tamar are viewed as foreigners.

I once arrived here during the 2002 World Cup. Of the 58,000 pubs in England, The Tinners appeared to be the only one not showing England's crucial second-round match.

An old black and white television was finally turned on and, through the static, I could hear low murmurs of approval from the locals every time an England attack broke down.

They were supporting Denmark. ✠

THE YEW TREE

CAULDON WATERHOUSES, STOKE-ON-TRENT, STAFFORDSHIRE, ST10 3EJ

NIGHT AT THE MUSEUM: ECCENTRIC PARADISE FOUND NEAR STOKE .

In the black fastness of a windy winter's evening, the traveller's spirits are lifted by the sight of The Yew Tree ('Turn left down the unmarked road, keep going past the cement works, you can't miss it,' explains a local). When we get there, we rendezvous with Alan Yates, a bow-tie-wearing bon viveur and the pub's landlord for, as he puts it, 'a mere forty-six years'.

There are no carpets at the Yew Tree, no bar meals and a distinct lack of alcopops. Music can be obtained from a symphonium for the princely sum of two pence. Scattered everywhere are vicious-looking agricultural items, grandfather clocks and vintage sheet music ranging from Verdi to Freddie Mercury (well, 'Bohemian Rhapsody'). It's a peculiar blend of twinkling bonhomie and faint, vestigial menace – you'd imagine Heath Robinson could fashion up a time machine out of ephemera that includes a boneshaker bicycle, a Jacobean four-poster bed and one of Queen Victoria's stockings. The oddness continues behind the bar. The till is pre-decimal, and the ancient beer pumps will warm the heart of anyone who remembers Double Diamond. On the wall is a bizarre musical instrument called a serpent.

'Roy Wood once played a tune on that,' says Alan. 'He lives locally.'

The great unsung genius of British pop in the country's most eccentric pub? Make up the camp bed, we're moving in. ⊹

No. 16

THE HEART & HAND

75 NORTH ROAD, BRIGHTON,
EAST SUSSEX, BN1 1YD

BRIGHTON ROCK: SOUTH COAST JUKEJOINT.

A magnet for writers, musicians and loafers in general, the H&H also serves as a handy field hospital for shell-shocked shoppers after an afternoon spent browsing the Lanes. Arrive here with frazzled nerves and you'll be reminded of what a good pub should be – a place for quiet contemplation and low-key conversation where no one looks up when you walk in the door.

If the exterior is impressive – an all-over façade of emerald green tiles that has remained unchanged for a hundred years – the inside is even more spectacular. On a sunny day, the stained-glass frontage bathes drinkers with a whisky-malt glow and you'll swear Jesus was an alcoholic.

The jewel in the crown? The vinyl-only jukebox, which appears to have come fully stocked after a clear-out at Keith Moon's house. Impervious to fashion and unaltered for at least fifteen years, it bears testimony to the longevity of the great pop single. Roll up day or night and you'll hear gems by Elvis, The Beach Boys or Hendrix interspersed with crackling 7" nuggets from the golden age of psych-pop: Love, The Small Faces, The 13th Floor Elevators. How many bands have formed or broken up to the sounds of Del Shannon's 'Runaway' blasting from these (im)perfect speakers?

Bonus ball: gaze upwards in the loo and you'll find pop-art originals on the cisterns.

The Heart & Hand: dissolute slumming; groovy plumbing.

STATION TO STATION

THE RISE AND FALL OF THE STATION PUB.

The train-station pub – less the journey's end, more the last chance saloon. Originally designed during a wave of mid-Victorian optimism as gleaming pit-stops for the thirsty traveller, by the late-seventies most of the nation's station pubs had, to paraphrase Bruce Robinson, taken on the jaundiced look of the inside of a lung.

Here, amid clouds of smoke, legions of solitary commuters would gather nightly, sucking on cheap cigarettes before heading back to the suburbs with a lukewarm bottle of Blue Nun and a Vesta curry for one (dinner inevitably in the dog back at base camp).

Rivalled only by airport pubs for encouraging a look of crumpled resignation*, these nicotine-heavy temples could tell a million stories of clandestine relationships and flunked promotion boards, the place where *Brief Encounter* finally met the Rovers Return.

Sadly, many of these alcoholic staging posts have either closed down or gone under the knife in the last thirty years. Across the country, sagging station pubs have been nipped 'n' tucked to cater for a new clientele more interested in a quick macchiato or M&S Simply Food than a two-course dinner of Carling and Capstan non-filters.

A fine example of traditional train station 'hospitality' was The Shires Bar at the old St Pancras terminus. Designed by William Barlow in 1868, the station occupied a huge arching room, one of the finest examples of Victorian Gothic architecture in the capital (just to add to the 'Release the Bats' credentials, it always seemed ten degrees colder than the rest of town). Like a spectacular weeping sore on the face of it stood The Shires.

With an atmosphere thick with smoke and the fug of general wrongdoing it was a magnet for every smack-head and ne'er do well in the NW1 area (and that was before the 'Football Special' pulled in). Here, tin ashtrays were nailed to the tables – you wonder who the hell would steal them, the nicotine stains could be carbon dated back to Brunel – and gaining access to the toilets involved a procedure worthy of Kafka. The drinks were so awful you almost felt like applauding. The place was like some brilliant, brutal art installation, the kind of thing that would walk away with the Turner Prize if faced with competition from a blinking lightbulb or some pottery made by a bloke in a dress.

Nowadays, of course, it's so different. The station, now home to Eurostar, proudly boasts the longest champagne bar in Europe. 'Imagine 1,372 Champagne flutes lined up side by side...' reads the literature. Food is of the canapé variety – salmon-roe blinis, you know the sort of thing, darling. The most expensive bottle of champagne is a staggering £2,500. In other words, it's a mighty long way from the happy horrors of The Shires.

In the Rough Pub Guide's hallucinatory vision for the refurbished station, things are very different. Our dream is to re-create a truer representation of the country; a vision that exists outside the station walls; where the champagne bar is replaced by the longest real-ale bar in the world. Inside, ancient horse harnesses give off an eye-watering smell that mixes Brasso and Kiwi shoe polish (think less Audrey

Hepburn in *Breakfast At Tiffany's*, more Audrey Roberts off Coronation Street).

Hand pumps would represent the ales of the four nations of the United Kingdom – from the Caledonian Brewery down to Cornwall's St Austell; from Adnams in the East to Ffos Y Ffin in West Wales. Food would be honest to goodness – Black Country Pork Scratchings, haggis, Welsh rarebit, bangers and mash, Neeps, tatties, and pies from Melton Mowbray.

Here a permanent workforce of all-day drinkers would be employed to prop up the bar, paid to talk loudly about football results rather than the results of that day's trading. Side by side in giant display cabinets would be row upon row of gleaming pint pots and personalised tankards – a lipstick-smudged wine glass or two at the end should act as discouragement enough from asking to see the cocktail list. The barmaids would be rosy cheeked and buxom, far more Argos than Selfridges, and drinks would top out at the £3 mark (hey, let's dream a little).

This would be the true gateway to the Rough Pub nation. This is what we've been denied. ✠

(*R.I.P. The Tap and Spile, the old airside bar at Heathrow.)

THE FREE TRADE INN

ST LAWRENCE ROAD, BYKER, NEWCASTLE, TYNE & WEAR, NE6 1AP

NO FT, NO COMMENT.

It's reassuring to know that some things don't change. The last ten years may have seen Newcastle transformed from a dowdy spinster into a sexy starlet – with the Gateshead Millennium Bridge as the ostentatious rock gleaming on its finger – but The Free Trade remains defiantly unkempt.

Described as 'a dump' by the *Observer* in 2002, The Free Trade is so unprepossessing that you can imagine stray Millwall fans – having wreaked havoc in Bigg Market – moving hurriedly along, terrified of what might lurk within.

Sadly, the free vinyl jukebox went the way of the Dodo in 2000, but the 'Drink Beer, Smoke Tabs' sign behind the bar still survives. The Trade retains a loyal following thanks to a local beer supply, a cracking CD jukebox (think Ween,

Pulp, Johnny Cash, Man or Astroman? – and that's just one CD) and unrivalled views over the Tyne. A trip to the toilets, meanwhile, will delight anyone who thinks pub graffiti is a dying art – they'll even lend you a biro at the bar if you ask nicely.

Jimi Hendrix, so it is said, took a shine to the place while staying with manager and ex-Animal Chas Chandler in nearby Heaton. Although rumours that an early hit started life as 'Stone Free (Trade)' may be pushing it.

THE ACE OF SPADES

BLOOMFIELD ROAD, TIPTON, DUDLEY, WEST MIDLANDS, DY4 9AJ

BORN TO BOOZE: MIDLANDS PREMIER ROCK PUB.

A hundred years ago, factory workers from the nearby steelworks would soothe their troubled brows with a pint of mild in Tipton local The Old Bush. A century on, and the sound of heavy metal remains as loud as ever.

The brainchild of Penny Hewitt and Andy Smith, The Ace of Spades – aka The Beer And Barrel – is the sort of no-holds-barred rock pub you'd imagine the young Ian 'Lemmy' Kilminster dreaming about. The wood-panelled snug features blue suede seats, the pool table is emblazoned with a Jack Daniel's logo and in the lounge bar the walls are a fetching shade of (what else?) deep purple.

On the walls, the cream of the Celestial All-Star Band (Elvis, Frank Zappa, Billy Fury, Janis Joplin) look down upon drinkers enjoying a menu boasting Black Country staples of faggots, grey peas and bacon.

Bikers are welcome, but The Ace also attracts some curious guests. Beer-mat artist AJW – who has been baffling drinkers in the Midlands since 1959 with his ink drawings of Mario Lanza – left his mark here last year. ✟

SPECIALLY PACKED FOR

ACE OF SPADES

Rock & Blues Bar
PORK SCRATCHINGS

Ingredients
Pork Rinds Salt, Flavour Enhancer (Monosodium Glutamate), Hydrolised Vegetable Protein, Flavourings.

Packed By : Whit Products Ltd
121 557 7651
www.sales@whitproducts.com

UK
FR 019
EC

Best Before 190808

080520

0501605080116

THE GREEN MAN

HARRODS, BELGRAVIA,
LONDON, SW1X 7XL

SHOW ME THE MOËT.

As licensee names above pub doors go, Mohamed Al Fayed's takes some beating. The notorious billionaire, owner of Harrods and Fulham Football Club, is the unlikely patron of The Green Man, a bijou boozer tucked away down in the depths of Harrods. Decked out entirely in polished wood and green leather, this is a pub that positively urges clandestine liaisons.

After navigating the labyrinthine ground floor to find the place (tip, use the Basil Street entrance to avoid the olfactory assault of the perfume hall) you find yourself at a proper bar where you can order pints, including a Harrods-own Czech-brewed lager (goes down a dream, like a Budvar or a Pilsner Urquell – one warning though, it doesn't come cheap). Plonk down among the curious mix of silent tourists and excitable couples and admire the décor. The walls are tastefully covered with antique maps of the counties of England – possibly to plant hot-headed ideas of places to elope to. Sixteenth-century Norfolk doesn't half look inviting. Sit back and soak it all in and realise that, above you, there are six floors of high-class shopping. Three pints in, contemplate testing out whether you can actually buy an elephant if you need one (we didn't see one in the food hall, not sure where else they'd be stocked?).

Whether a pub in a shop should count for this guide is questionable – the place has the feel of a film set and is dangerously close to the men's hair saloon. That said, for somewhere to come, booze and live out dizzying fantasies of ditching London life for something more outré, The Green Man opens up a world of possibilities. Well, maybe just the world of a pre-Land Act East Anglia… ⚜

THE ELLANGOWAN HOTEL

ST JOHN STREET, CREETOWN,
DUMFRIES AND GALLOWAY, DG8 7JF

PAGAN FERTILITY RITES A SPECIALITY.

We've all had the conversation: when your mates come back from an ill-thought-out weekend in the country. And no matter where they have visited, they always refer to the local pub as being like 'something out of *The Wicker Man*', that classic 1970s' horror movie where Edward Woodward is mocked and eventually burned alive by rural Scottish islanders.

Well, if you ever find yourself in Creetown then you can drink in a bar that actually is something out of *The Wicker Man*. Because the Ellangowan Hotel bar was used by the film's makers as the set for The Green Man pub in the movie. Getting there early is advised, in order to meet OAP locals Willie, Jimmy and Billy, who set up at the bar at around half eight in the morning to get to work on their force-twelve booze habit.

The locals are obviously proud of the bar's cinematic connections and enjoy baiting visitors by hitting them over the head with metals spoons that they also use to play tunes from the film. Families of actual Pagans from as far afield as Tasmania visit the bar to pay homage to the movie, which can lead to some disconcerting conversations. Traditional Scottish hospitality is rife, as we discovered when we looked for the gents but accidentally opened the entrance to the kitchen.

'Wrong door, prick!' shouted out a helpful regular. ✠

THE PILCHARD INN

BURGH ISLAND, BIGBY-ON-SEA, DEVON, TQ7 4BG

DEVON IS A PLACE ON EARTH.

In the past, Burgh Island has provided a picturesque haven for Agatha Christie (who wrote some Poirot books here), J.M.W. Turner (who painted here) and The Beatles (who escaped here after a gig in Plymouth). Much more interesting for us, though, is the island's small but perfectly formed public house, The Pilchard Inn.

When The Pilchard is cut off from the mainland it is only accessible by a sea tractor, a high-rise contraption that looks like something the A-Team would have built to bust out of a very low-rise problem. With the waves massaging the shoreline, the pub becomes a haven of tranquillity, providing the setting for easily the most sublime pint in the country. The place is tiny – a cosy, heavily beamed room for visitors and a snug bar built around a hypnotic fire for hotel residents and Pilchard regulars from the mainland. This being south Devon, you're pretty much guaranteed sitting-out weather all summer.

To add to the beautiful mystique of the place, the spirits here aren't just of the drinking kind – the pub is said to be haunted by a handful of different ghosts (collectively christened Tom Crocker by the bar staff, after a smuggler who was allegedly shot there by customs officers) – expect the odd disturbance, but nothing so bad as to put you off your ale (which is all sourced locally and incredible). The whole experience has the same meditative effect as a week's island hopping around the Med, allowing you to unwind to a beautiful point of merrily pissed stupor, helping you forget the crap that's happening back on the mainland.

It's as close to heaven in a public house as you can get. ✠

GEORGE BEST

'I spent a lot of money on booze, birds and fast cars. The rest I just squandered.'

KEITH MOON

'Everybody I know is a drinker. I've met most of my best friends in pubs.'

VIVIAN STANSHALL

'If I had all the money I've spent on drink, I'd spend it on drink.'

PETER COOK

'If people think they are more interesting than a cigarette then they must be truly arrogant.'

SAMUEL JOHNSON

'Claret is the liquor for boys; port for men; but he who aspires to be a hero must drink brandy.'

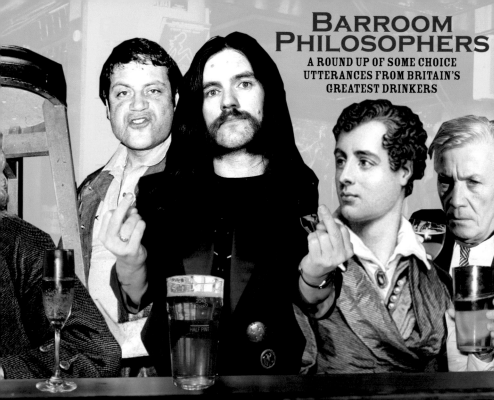

BARROOM PHILOSOPHERS

A ROUND UP OF SOME CHOICE UTTERANCES FROM BRITAIN'S GREATEST DRINKERS

OLIVER REED

'What's the point of staying sober?'

LEMMY

'Why do I drink? I like the taste. I don't get hangovers because I don't stop drinking. I don't get drunk either. I just carry on then do it again. When I wake up in the morning I drink a coke with something in it and I take it from there.'

LORD BYRON

'Let us have wine and women, mirth and laughter. Sermons and soda water the day after.'
'Man, being reasonable, must get drunk; the best of life is but intoxication.'

JEFFREY BERNARD

'Oh, to me, not drinking is like being dead, almost. I sit here taking endless journeys down memory lane. It gets boring.'

ROUGH PUB TOP TEN

10 MARISCO TAVERN
9   BAIRDS BAR
8   THE VULCAN
7   THE FOUNDRY
6   THE LEWES ARMS
5   CRAZY SCOTS
4   WILKINS CIDER FARM
3   THE TEMPLE
2   THE DYFFRYN ARMS
1   THE MONTAGUE ARMS

THE MARISCO TAVERN

LUNDY, EX39 2LY

PINT OF NO RETURN: THE MOST ISOLATED PUB IN ENGLAND.

There's another Devon pub stuck out there on an island, a completely different beast to The Pilchard. The Marisco Tavern on Lundy must deserve the title of the South of England's most isolated pub. Lying 12 miles off the coast of North Devon, Lundy is a granite outcrop measuring 3.5 miles by 0.5 miles. A sanctuary for wildlife, it attracts all manner of twitchers and ramblers. On a clear day you can see the Gower Peninsula and the blue-flag beach at Woolacombe. Getting there took three attempts, as crossings were cancelled at the last minute due to unfavourable conditions but, eventually, the beer gods smiled down on us, calmed the waves and let the Balmoral pleasure cruiser park up for two-and-a-half hours of shore leave.

Like the rest of the island The Marisco is managed by the Landmark Trust. It sits 130m above sea level, a boozy eyrie atop the rock. Unless you're pretty much lame, you're walking up – or, in this case, sprinting, in order to be first at the bar.

Inside, it's rammed full of mariner's detritus and the kind of seating that feels like shelter from an oncoming storm. There are two glorious beers brewed specifically for the island by St Austell in Cornwall. When you've drunk them, the view from the roofless gents toilets is an endless horizon of rolling sea.

Although the feeling of utter isolation while sat in the silent boozer is odd at first, it doesn't take long to begin zoning out properly and starting to contemplate missing the only boat out of here for the next four days – all it took was three swift pints before I needed to be physically dragged back to the jetty, the last one onboard.

Yeah, it's really good here. I could get quite into the island life. ✠

BAIRDS BAR

224–226 GALLOWGATE, GLASGOW, G4 0TS

BHOYS ZONE: GLASGOW'S GREENEST PUB.

As abrasive as a drunken docker and just as volatile, Bairds Bar looms from out of the mists of Gallowgate and demands respect. A shrine to Celtic Football Club, Bairds is a place where loyalty to the cause is tattooed on every forearm and where any Scottish or Irish connections should be flagged up as quickly as possible.

Along the walls scarves, flags and vintage shirts tell of distant campaigns dating back to the days of Jimmy McGrory. Behind the bar, a replica of the European Cup won by the Lisbon Lions in 1967 reminds visitors from south of the border not to get too cocky. If a poster of The Beatles doctored so that they're wearing Celtic kit is plain daft, you didn't hear us saying it.

Visitors from Tunbridge Wells may not appreciate a conversational flow that could make Gordon Ramsay blush, but they should think themselves lucky. Approach this impregnable pea-green fortress wearing a Rangers shirt and you'll feel about as comfortable as an Arabic despatch rider pressing the doorbell of the White House.

At Bairds strangers are treated with the same roughhouse good humour of a grizzly bear playing with a kitten. Within seconds of arrival a bloke at the bar informs me he's a mercenary who did ten years in the Foreign Legion.

'Keep your sense of humour or you'll die,' he says, hinting at a decade of knocking off Algerians. Another is keen to sell me pornographic videos.

Enjoy the banter, but you'll never fit in.

For Celtic fans, Bairds is an idyll to match The Shire, and for rivals, Mordor. The rest of us are just watching the movie. ✠

THE VULCAN

10 ADAM STREET,
CARDIFF, CF24 2FH

Sometimes things just don't make sense. If you looked up the definition of 'perfect city-centre pub', there would be a picture of The Vulcan Hotel in Cardiff right next to it. No nonsense and unreconstructed, The Vulcan is beautifully tiled outside, warm and wooden inside. Sawdust is scattered on the floor in front of the dartboard. The jukebox is determinedly anti-fashion – The Rockford Files theme blasts out before 'Whiskey in the Jar'. Affable Cardiffians sit drinking Brains SA, which has travelled less than a mile from the brewery to be here. The landlady – a lovely, vivacious Welsh lass – stands you a drink before you can fish your wallet out. What's the problem then?

The Vulcan now stands alone on Adam Street. After over 150 years as a pub,

its future is now seriously threatened. Although currently reprieved until mid-2009, the talk is that the site will eventually be turned into a car park. Local Liberal Democrat councillors have rallied around The Vulcan in a bid to save it, but there is already talk of reassembling it brick by brick in the Museum of Welsh Life in nearby St Fagans. Let's just hope it doesn't come to that.

The Vulcan, one of Cardiff's oldest pubs, should be protected as a listed building. Without somewhere like this existing for future generations, people will think that the only places we boozed in were Irish theme bars that had a crèche attached. At the end of the day, though, this really just comes down to a question of whether commerce is more important than local heritage.

You should already know where we stand on that one.

No. 7
THE FOUNDRY

84–86 GREAT EASTERN STREET,
LONDON, EC2A 3JL

PUB WITH AN ARTISTIC LICENCE.

Perched on a traffic island at the edge of the trendy Shoreditch Triangle sits The Foundry, London's most out-there boozer. Looking like a squat populated by alcoholic art students, The Foundry occupies two floors of an old bank with an almost-violent disregard for the building's original usage. The toilets are so deep in graffiti it takes you a minute to work out which is the gents; neon signs glow with a warm, headache-inducing buzz; music ranges from the kind of glitchy dubstep – that sounds like someone drilling into your forehead – to Dolly Parton's *Greatest Hits* played off scratchy well-worn vinyl.

Occupying a weird no-man's-land between 'art happening' and local pub (the pub stocks beer from the Pitfield Brewery that used to stand less than 50 yards up the road), The Foundry seems to exist to make people think while they drink. The centrepiece of the upstairs bar is a large framed piece of text by Bill Drummond (of the KLF/K Foundation) inviting punters to try their hand. With suitable élan, it reads 'I Could Fuckin' Do Better Than That'.

Basically, you're a long way from Wetherspoon's here.

By the bar, the walls are plastered with pictures of patrons from years gone by – a veritable Rogues' Gallery of drunkards, ne'er do wells, artists and dropouts. Stare long enough and you'll see pictures of Irvine Welsh and Gavin Turk in there, alongside Tony Benn talking to a rapt audience sat in the middle of room, seemingly at home among the wonderful and provocative carnage that is The Foundry. Quite what Anthony Wedgwood would make of the 'artworks' currently on display is beyond us though… ⊬

THE LEWES ARMS

MOUNT PLACE, LEWES,
EAST SUSSEX, BN7 1YH

STRONG ENOUGH TO SURVIVE BEER GROUP PRESSURE.

The Lewes Arms came to public attention last year when locals successfully ran their 'Hands off our Harveys' campaign, lobbying the Greene King brewery for the return of their favourite pint, brewed less than half a mile from here. A front-page story on the *Guardian* featured a man picketing outside, dressed up in demented regalia with his face painted green in protest. Point taken, normal service was resumed. Except, at this beautiful, welcoming backstreet pub, 'service' is anything but normal. Wilfully eccentric is the best possible way to describe it, the pub has been host to the World Pea Throwing competition, Shakespearean lap-dancing nights (think Showgirls with added sonnets),

dog fashion parades ('Not the kind of dog fashion you're thinking of!' it's helpfully pointed out) and celebrations of the local tradition of Dwyle Flunking, which involves dancing, merriment and throwing booze-soaked rags at a volunteer. Restoration Day, held annually on 26 April to celebrate the date that the pub's beloved bitter was brought back, is an event marked with a torch-lit march around the surrounding streets and much singing – exactly the kinds of things that local boozers should be encouraging more of.

The Lewes Arms is the perfect example of a 'community pub' – somewhere where like-minded individuals can go and actually enjoy themselves – to talk and to socialise; to drink and to laugh – massively underrated pub activities these days.

Power to the people indeed! ⊹

No. 5

THE CRAZY SCOTS BAR

9 RIGBY ROAD, BLACKPOOL,
LANCASHIRE, FY1 5DE

SMOKE ON THE WATER.

J.B. Priestley once described Blackpool as 'a great roaring spangled beast'. Walking along the seafront on a Saturday afternoon, it makes you wonder who could ever hold the lead. As brassy as Bette Lynch and as hedonistic as Pete Doherty, it's a tanked-up Tinseltown where cheap perfume and strong lager mix on the breeze and a rebellious spirit ferments.

Nowhere is this refusal to toe the line more evident than at The Crazy Scots because, despite the best efforts of Gordon Brown, Patricia Hewitt and health fascists nationwide, this is the only pub in Britain where you can still smoke without shivering in a doorway.

'People work hard all week and, at the end of it, they have one small pleasure – a pint and a fag,' explains landlord Hamish Howitt. 'Who has the right to deny them

that? Thirty-two per cent of the population smoke in Blackpool and, since the ban, they aren't allowed to gather in one place. Apply these measures to any other minority group and there would be uproar.'

As a result of Hamish's one-man campaign, The Crazy Scots – formerly a bustling karaoke bar – now doubles as HQ for the newly formed UK FAGS Party (an acronym for Fight Against Government Suppression). Banners reading: 'Smokescreen', and 'Curfew! Fourteen million smokers under house arrest' cover the outside of the building. Bar staff wear 'Save Hamish' T-shirts bearing the legend: 'You can still smoke in gaol'. There are even plans to hoist a 20ft inflatable of a glowing cigarette on the roof, which will give new meaning to the phrase 'lighting up the skies'.

The combined effect feels more like an ideological stronghold from the Miners'

Why is no-one standing up for working-class rights?

● ight
● gainst
● overnment
● uppression

Tony Blair and his PC Correct Luvvie Brigade think Socialism is a designer aftershave!

uk-fags is a REGISTERED POLITICAL PARTY

www.uk-fags.co.uk

Little Britain Little Dictators

Yeah Butt! No Butt!
Yeah Butt!
NO BUTTS!

Strike or Paris '68 than a pub a stone's throw from the Golden Mile.

'This isn't about smoking,' says Hamish. 'I don't even smoke myself. It's about the nanny state telling people what they can and can't do. The ban is an erosion of our basic civil liberties.'

Inevitably, there's been a price to pay for flouting the law so publicly. Trade has tailed off and the outlook is bleak.

'A lot of my regulars can't afford to risk getting a £50 fine and a criminal record, so they stay away,' says Hamish. 'Three nights a week the council come down here and tell me that I should be closed. But I'll take this all the way to the European Court of Human Rights.'

He smiles ruefully.

'I'll go to prison over this if I have to.'

To register your support for Hamish, visit www.uk-fags.co.uk. ✠

WILKINS CIDER FARM

LAND'S END, MUDGLEY,
SOMERSET, BS28 4TU

THE CIDER HOUSE RULES.

To find the source of the best cider in the West Country, its bubbling spring of thick, fermented apple juice, you'll need a bit of patience. Here, in the Vale of Avalon, where the lanes are lined with unkempt hedges that sprawl up to obscure dizzying twists and turns in the road, signposts become increasingly scarce. When you eventually find Land's End, you'll hit paydirt – the Wilkins Cider Farm.

Roger Wilkins took over cider brewing on this working dairy farm thirty-nine years ago. Now aged sixty, he's as fit as a butcher's dog, this despite of (or possibly because of)

the fact that he drinks anything up to fourteen pints of his potent brew a day. His cider and hospitality is so legendary that Joe Strummer moved to the tiny hamlet of Mudgley just so that he could be nearer to the farm. Strummer was known to stay drinking all night, often to be found by friends in the early hours talking to the moon. Pictures on the wall of John Lydon clutching a brimming glass with his arm around Roger only manage to seal the farm's punk-rock credentials.

The cider farm is simplicity itself. Four huge cider barrels – two dry, two sweet – dominate the room. There really is no point heading down here for a nice Bordeaux or a Fosters Super Chilled.

declaring them like drinking 'sugar water' – after all, he says: 'If you want cider, you've got to drink it rough!'

After a few glasses you're pretty woozy with the warm, slightly psychedelic glow you just don't get from any other booze. Roger sorts us out 20 litres of take out and our designated driver fires up the engine for the return to reality. It's at this point when I realise just why Strummer moved here to spend wistful days drinking on the farm and long nights in conversation with the planets and the stars above. It's because the Wilkins Cider Farm serves up easily the most cosmic pint in Britain.

There are some cheeses, pickles and crisps on sale to help mop up the booze. The 'snug' is a white room in a converted barn with a few scattered chairs and a sofa that seems to swallow you up when you collapse into it. In the rafters, a family of starlings chirrup away. Roger is talking to some locals about 'modern' ciders,

No. 3

THE TEMPLE

GREAT BRIDGEWATER STREET,
MANCHESTER, M1 5JW

**GOING UNDERGROUND: BAR BASED IN
EX-PUBLIC TOILET.**

What makes for the perfect pub?
Unpretentious atmosphere and friendly
service? Check. A drinks list that features
all of the great beer-brewing nations of
the world? Of course. A jukebox that
effortlessly covers the last forty years of
rock 'n' roll history? Absolutely. Toilet
walls decorated with black
and white 1950s' erotica?
Well, that goes without
saying. Sometimes, though,
you end up finding this
kind of perfection in the
strangest of places. The
Temple, located in the
beating heart of Manchester,
ticks all those boxes, yet is
housed in a converted public
convenience.

While a lot of venues get sneeringly
labelled 'toilets', this place wears that
tag as a badge of pride. Pretty much the
archetypal Northern dive bar, The Temple
is a windowless, subterranean room with
seating for no more than thirty people, yet
it has the feel of a wonderfully pissed-up
clubhouse, the kind of place where days
spiral into nights and then on into the
following week. Presided over by Scott
Alexander, an Aussie ex-
pat who you're likely to see
cradling his pet dog in his
arms as he lines up shots
on the bar, The Temple
is one of Manchester's
greatest bars – albeit one
set in what was once one of
the city's most-notorious
cottaging haunts. This
place sets the bog standard
to an all-time high.

THE DYFFRYN ARMS
(A.K.A. BESSIE'S)

GWAUN VALLEY ROAD, PONTFAEN, DYFED, SA65 9SG

ROLL OUT THE BARREL.

A truly great pub is as much about its atmosphere and its place in the community as it is about the beer it serves. The Dyffryn Arms serves only one beer, yet has been a stalwart of every single *CAMRA Good Beer Guide* (bar the first edition back in 1973). It also recently made their National Inventory of Historic Interiors – the pub equivalent of becoming a Grade I listed building. The pub, known locally as Bessie's, is situated above the Landsker Line in the Gwaun Valley in Pembrokeshire. It has been run by the titular landlady (now in her eighties) for nearly fifty years. Here, she dishes up Bass straight from the barrel through a serving hatch in the back wall. If Bessie isn't already at the bar, you bang on an empty Taffy Apples cider bottle for service.

The inside hasn't really been touched since the 1920s – a poster of the Prince of Wales is actually the 1910 version and not HRH Charlie Windsor (when Bessie mentions that the pub has been visited by the Prince, you're not quite sure which one she means). The only touch of modernity has been a coat of paint on the ceiling to remove the orange gloss of years of nicotine staining. On a sunny day you can sit on one of the benches out front and take a deep hit of the green, green grass of the valley. Village life here in Pontfaen revolves around the front bar of Bessie's and probably always will. This is a local pub for local people. And that's a brilliant thing. ⊹

H.R.H. THE PRINCE OF WALES

For Sale
Terror of Pirates

THE MONTAGUE ARMS

289 QUEENS ROAD, NEW CROSS,
LONDON, SE15 2PA

ALES OF THE UNEXPECTED.

First-time visitors to The Montague Arms are often overwhelmed by the random nature of the décor. What is a (real) human skeleton doing perched on the bar? Why is an embalmed zebra peering out from inside a horse-drawn carriage? And are the Penny Farthing, antique muskets and diving helmet prizes in some surrealist interpretation of The Generation Game?

Like a seventeenth-century galleon shipwrecked in SE15, The Montague has long been marvelled over by coach parties from Jersey to Japan, benefactors of its position as an ideal pit-stop for drivers headed towards the A2 to Dover. As a result, its legend has spread far and wide since landlord Peter Hoyle took over the reins in 1967.

Originally 'full of gangsters', Peter set about reinventing the pub as a community-minded local with an emphasis on live music. Sporting velvet loon pants, a paisley shirt and a bushy ginger beard, drummer Peter and (blind) organist Peter London would entertain crowds with covers of everything from The Bee Gees' 'Massachusetts' to Neil Young's 'After The Goldrush', with a moog-assisted rendition of 'Macarthur Park' as the show-stopper (captured on 1971's cabaret

had told him about the pub, he insisted they come straight from the airport. Paul got up and played a load of hits.'

Since a nautical makeover in 1978, little at The Montague has changed. The bar staff – now in their seventies – sip sherry and natter with an all-ages clientele, while if there's the occasional squawk of appreciation, blame it on Snowy the parrot who lives upstairs.

Every Saturday night 'The Two Petes' still play and, in this scruffy corner of South London, a pub spirit dating back to the Blitz holds sway. On New Year's Eve 2007 their repertoire included 'The Lambeth Walk', 'Life On Mars' and 'Wonderwall'. It was free to get in, everyone sang and danced and a good time was had by all. Fairy lights twinkled off the skeleton on the bar.

You really had to be there. Hopefully next year, you will. ✣

classic Live At The Ever New Montague Arms, available on-line here: http://blog.wfmu.org/freeform/2007/07/365-days-195---.html.

During the 1980s, everyone from Mike 'Runaround' Reid to a Beatle graced the stage, despite it often boasting a bucket for rain leaks.

'One night Paul McCartney walked in the door,' laughs Peter. 'He'd met Jim Davidson on the plane and, after Jim

'THEY ALSO SERVED'

WHAT NEXT FOR THE GREAT BRITISH BOOZER?

Wondering what that clanging sound is you've been hearing in pub land over the last couple of years? That'll be the pre-emptive death-knell for the boozer being rung out. Whether it's down to the depressing dominance of the colossal Pubcos (the biggest three of whom own over 20,000 licensed establishments in the UK)

or Chancellor Alistair Darling (now effectively banned from every pub in the United Kingdom) balancing the Budget with a pure kick-in-the-balls beer tax, the Draconian smoking ban, dirt cheap supermarket booze or just the plain old nagging threat of an impending recession, it seems everything is conspiring against the good old-fashioned local.

It's the same up and down the country. Everywhere you go you see boarded-up pubs. Some will be reborn as expensive cocktail bars, many as family-friendly gastropubs, while some will face the worst fate of all – being gutted out and refitted for sale as flats and offices. The British Beer and Pub Association estimated that 1,409 pubs closed in 2007, while Iain Loe from CAMRA notes it's not just the city centres that are suffering. 'For the first time since the Domesday Book, more than half our villages are without a pub,' (the *Observer*, 20 April, 2008). With much current buzz talk among the chattering classes of

local distinctiveness, it actually seems that we're in a very real danger of becoming distinctly local-less.

What can be done to plug the hole in the dam short of taking up residence, *Shaun of the Dead*-style, and fighting off the zombie hordes of redevelopers and bureaucrats who seem determined to squeeze the last few bits of genuine fun out of life? What can any of us really do to ensure that the taps keep flowing?

Well, if there is an underlying point to this book it's that there are still plenty of places left out there that defy the prevailing 'anti-pub' forces – all you have

to do is look for them and then cherish them. In the case of somewhere like The Vulcan (see pages 142–145) you might not have too long left to raise a glass, but that doesn't mean it's not worth making the trek and paying your respects because, let's face it, there are few things more disheartening than turning up somewhere with a thirst on and a well-thumbed guidebook in hand to see the words 'Closed For Business' writ large over the windows.

At the time of writing there are, according to the British Beer and Pub Association, approximately 57,500 pubs in the UK. By CAMRA's most conservative estimates, fifty-seven are closing their doors for good every month. In these pages, we're vouching for fifty British classics. The rest – well, that's where you, the denizens of the Rough Pub country, come in! ⌖

PSSST...

CREDIT WHERE CREDIT IS DUE

MILDMAY ROAD CREW, SOPH, CHRIS & JONATHAN

PJT + TINA + BEN

DEEK, EMS & CARL

HUW, ALL HIS GIRLS & ALL OF AUSTRALIA – ROUGH PUB HEAVEN

MATT TURNER

NATHAN DETROIT

MARIE + THE SOCIAL & ALL WHO SAIL IN HER

JEFF, MART, SPENCE, ANDREW, DAN & ALL HEAVENLY BODIES

PICTURE CREDITS: ALLSTAR 1, AQUARIUS COLLECTION 35, 65, 67, BFI 127, LFI 27, THE KOBAL COLLECTION 68, MIRROR PIX 37, SCOPE FEATURES 33, 34, SOLENT 57.

COMPILED & EDITED
BY PAUL MOODY
& ROBIN TURNER

PHOTOGRAPHY BY
SCOTT WISHART

ESIGNED BY RUSSELL MOORCROFT

PLUS SPECIAL
THANKS TO...
**IAN PREECE
(AND ALL AT ORION)**

SIMON BENHAM

ADDITIONAL
PHOTOGRAPHY
AND EDITORIAL
NEIL THOMSON

ER UNDER THE
BRIDGE

MAM

THE
RATS
GET
FAT
WHILE
BRAVE
EN

EANOR xxx

JANE

BEG
CLAIRE + JAMIE

JAKE
LINGWOOD

ALL AT
CAT HILL
**THE
CHRIS PENN
SUITE**

JET

Afterword

When we started writing about our favourite old pubs in the first issue of *Socialism* back in 2004, the pub trade was in comparatively rude health. Five years on, and barely a day goes by without a newspaper headline or a TV bulletin sounding the death knell for the traditional local. To this end, we'd like to know your thoughts on the best pubs in Britain. Do you know somewhere we should have included?

If you do, please email us at: **www.roughpubguide.co.uk**

Remember, a pub isn't just for Christmas, it's for life.

Cheers! ⚜

INDEX

Acknowledgements & thanks

Kate O'Neill at The Fox & Hounds, Jonathan and Tracey at The Foundry, Jason Chinnery, Jim Saunders, John Commons, Bob Beech, Jonathan Cole, Mike Taylor, Peter Simpson, Iain Salisbury, Gary Chilvers, Steve Lowe, and all the men of The Jockey Morris, Michael Tierney and The Handlebar Club, Ron Crabtree, Kieran Evans, Alan Yates, Mike at The Free Trade, Scott at The Temple, Guy Garvey, Dave Rofe, Sean Cook, Roger Wilkins, Liz at The Vulcan, James Dean Bradfield, Penny and Andy at The Ace Of Spades, Hamish Howitt (keep fighting the good fight!), all at The Montague, Gladys at The Palm Tree, Jamie Bowman, Lisa Southern, Alex Needham and everyone else who suggested pubs which never made the cut. Last but not least, you for reading this far. We owe you a pint.

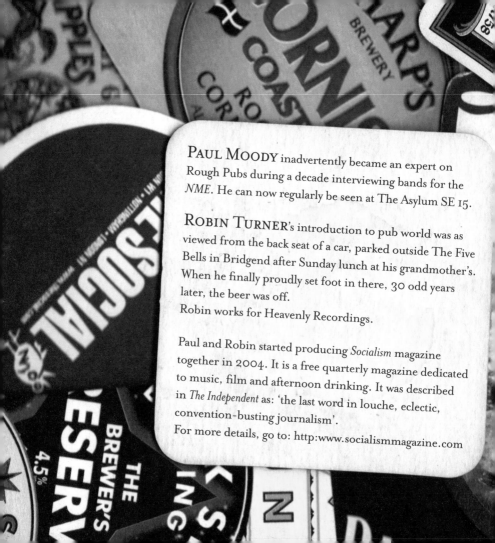

PAUL MOODY inadvertently became an expert on Rough Pubs during a decade interviewing bands for the *NME*. He can now regularly be seen at The Asylum SE 15.

ROBIN TURNER's introduction to pub world was as viewed from the back seat of a car, parked outside The Five Bells in Bridgend after Sunday lunch at his grandmother's. When he finally proudly set foot in there, 30 odd years later, the beer was off.
Robin works for Heavenly Recordings.

Paul and Robin started producing *Socialism* magazine together in 2004. It is a free quarterly magazine dedicated to music, film and afternoon drinking. It was described in *The Independent* as: 'the last word in louche, eclectic, convention-busting journalism'.
For more details, go to: http:www.socialismmagazine.com